Love Yourself

and Other Insurgent Acts
That Recast Everything

Copyright © 2019 Dushka Zapata

All rights reserved

ISBN: 9781704806488

This book's cover design is by Erin Pinkley.

This book has sand all over it.

I hope you build a castle with it.

To Erin, my accomplice in any apocalypse.

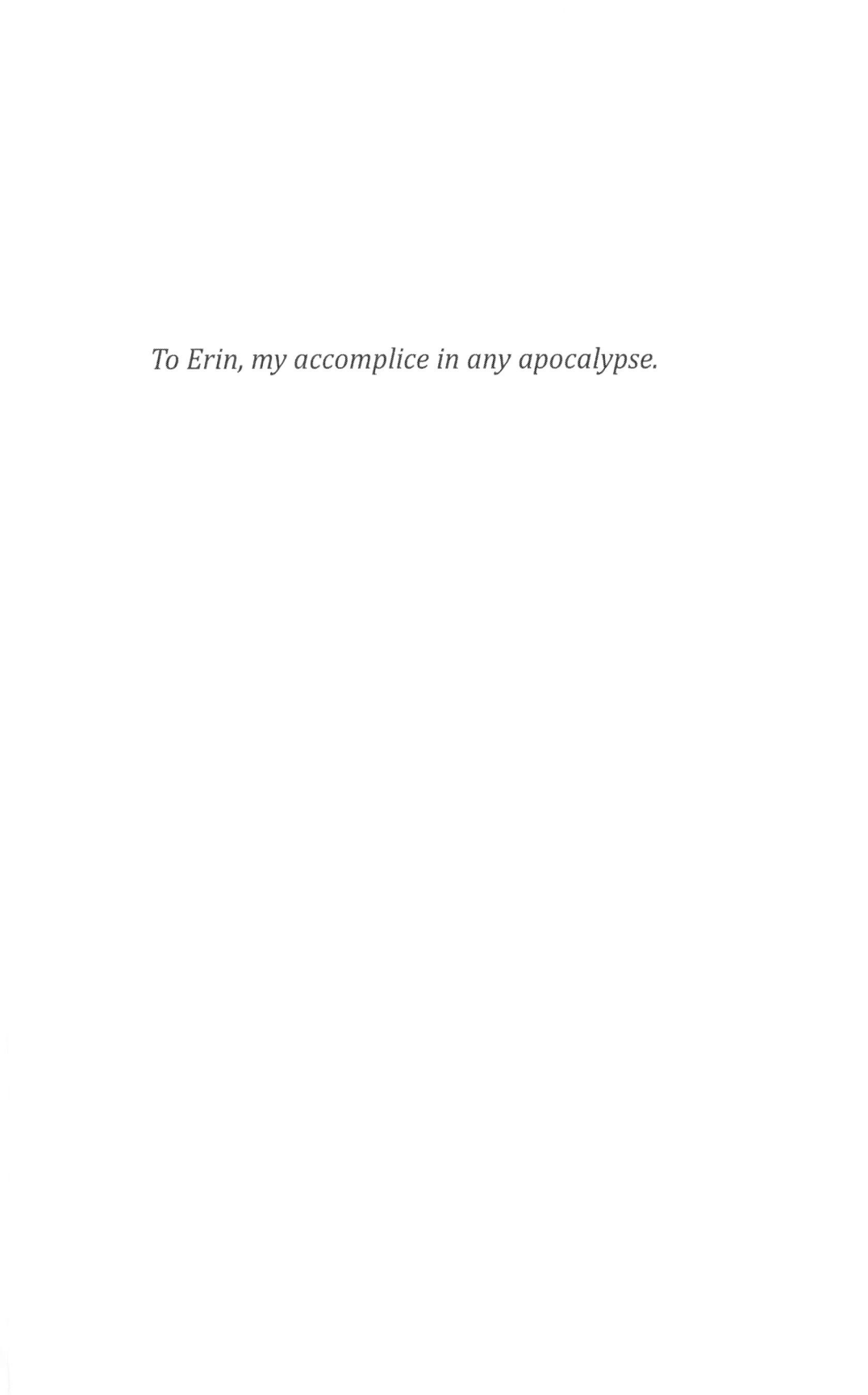

Author's Note:

I make it a point in each of my books to not repeat the same essays.

This book, however, has two or three essays that have appeared in other books.

This is because this book is intended as a "how to" manual.

Learning to love yourself is the adventure of a lifetime. I wanted you to have the relevant information available in a single place.

Any reference to time across the book "a month ago, a week ago", respects when the essay was written.

Contents

Love Yourself	1
Things to Keep in Mind Before Starting a Relationship	53
Things to Remember During a Relationship	129
Breaking Up and the Aftermath	235

Love Yourself

What I'm Looking For

When I was in my early teens I had a mad crush on a boy.

The subject of my love (the boy) changed pretty regularly.

What remained constant was the mad crush.

I felt like I would do anything to make him happy. I loved every little thing about him, even his quirks. I wanted to give him everything.

Until I lost interest, met another boy and began again.

The thrill and devastation of the mad crush roller coaster.

One day, in that vast, cold, gray, dry, empty expanse between one crush and another, I wondered if I had ever felt that mad love for myself.

Would I do anything to make me happy? Could I love every little thing about me, even my quirks? Would I give me anything?

I decided it was time to set aside the boy crushes and instead nurture a new kind of love. It seemed like a better investment of my time and energy to love someone I would always have by me, who would never neither bore me nor leave me.

Thus began a shift in my perspective.

I wasn't dieting because a boy wanted me to be thinner. I was eating better because I wanted to be healthy. I was taking care of myself.

If someone wasn't sure how they felt for me or wanted me to be someone I wasn't, rather than wanting to cling and desperately figure out how I could make them love me, I instead felt I deserved better.

I stopped being interested in those who weren't interested in me.

Instead of wondering how on earth I could be good enough to deserve someone's unconditional love I became pickier about who I loved. This selectiveness did not come from a place of arrogance but from a place of self-esteem.

I became more comfortable with uncertainty because I trusted I could probably figure out how to deal with whatever happened next.

I began to believe in myself, because that's what you do when you love someone.

I have learned the importance of spending time alone because I need to reduce background noise so I can listen to myself. How am I feeling? What do I need? What is it that I'm trying to tell me?

I recognize where I need help and give myself the space and the tools to bolster those areas without judgement and without being hard on myself. For example, I have a tendency towards anxiety, so I search for things that calm me (I try to go to yoga several times a week and pay attention to how I'm breathing).

I try to be what I am looking for. I want to be loved with a love that is true and deep and stable. I want someone who will always want what is best for me. I want someone I can count on.

That's what I work on becoming for myself.

Why Is It Bad to Need People?

Life is a great expedition across vast, varied terrain.

You embark upon it with a team you must rely on. Someone might be a map expert, another a master at predicting meteorological conditions. There are doctors and anthropologists and philosophers and storytellers. There are chefs and architects and poets, comedians and actors, liars and kings.

You all need each other. You are highly unlikely to survive this expedition all on your own.

At the same time, you are each responsible for carrying your own supplies. You shoulder your tent and food and water and anything else you define as necessary. Beauty. Harmony. Happiness. A soft blanket. Your special coffee cup.

One day, your pack feels really heavy. You just can't carry it anymore. You ask someone on the team to carry it for you.

Even if they say yes, this arrangement is not sustainable. It means they have to carry your things in addition to their own.

If you are not able to take responsibility for your own necessary supplies, sooner or later you become a burden, even to the people who love you the most.

With the decision of handing the things you should be responsible for to another, you jeopardize not only your own survival but the survival of others.

This is the difference between needing someone, which is inevitable, and being dependent on them. The first is natural, rhythmical, indispensable.

The second does not end well.

On My Own Terms

Do you know what I want?

I want to live life on my own terms.

I want to stop doing things because everyone does them and start doing things because they work for me and are true to who I am.

I need to stop asking myself if I am normal, and start asking myself what it is that will contribute to my sense of inner peace and my happiness.

Be less worried about fitting in and more about putting myself in a position where I can be of service to others in a way that is consistent with what I love.

I want expression. I want to create.

Any minute I spend struggling to be ordinary is time I don't spend living a life that — for me — serves some sort of purpose.

I don't care. I don't care if what I have recognized as something I want for myself is normal or not. What matters is that I have identified it.

This is no small thing.

Why Don't I Fit Into How the World Works?

There is no "way the world works".

You live in a world of worlds, worlds that are so alike they overlap, worlds so different and distant it's a wonder you can even make out their borders at all.

All these worlds exist in the same time, the same place, the same dimension.

They are all right here.

The way to find your world, where the population is your tribe, your clan, your crowd, is to step into who you are instead of making an effort to fit in.

As you do this — as you express your personality, your preferences, your choices, clarify your demands, outline your boundaries, as you are willing to let others down to stay true to yourself — the world where you belong makes itself increasingly evident and bright.

If you lament that you don't fit in but spend a lot of time trying, if you do what you do because it's what others do and not because you think you should, if you make choices in an effort to please, then your world sits close by but just beyond your grasp, invisible, locked behind a door you cannot open, because the only key is the full expression of yourself.

Find yourself, find your world.

Signs That You Need to Love Yourself

I need external validation — it's how I define myself.

I constantly compare myself to others.

I feel lost and can't tell the difference between "we" and "me".

I put others down.

I change a lot depending on who I'm with.

I don't let others see me.

Being alone makes me uncomfortable.

I blame.

A lot of the things I go through I seem to be going through again and again.

I take criticism really hard.

Navigating difficult emotions is almost intolerable.

I experience difficulty setting boundaries.

I assume that the way people act towards me is about me.

I make commitments towards myself and don't follow through.

I don't take care of myself.

I do unhealthy things that hurt me.

I talk to myself in ways I would never talk to anyone else.

I cannot trust others.

I'm never proud of me.

Proud

One of my favorite feelings is to feel proud of myself.

I used to keep this expansive sensation a secret. It's not cool, I realized, to reveal it because it's interpreted as a lack of modesty, as an absence of humility, as arrogance. It's not modest.

So I took a closer look.

By feeling proud of myself, I don't mean boastful. I don't mean an ego trip. I mean the realization that I did something I frankly didn't think I could.

I am not coming from a place of conceit but rather from a place of recognition and identity.

It's not that I'm hot stuff — it's that I am able.

Call me cocky, but there are many, many things I've done that I never in a million years thought I could and I'm really quite impressed with this person living inside of me.

In a world where people are quick to cut you down to size, to bring you down a notch, I think this sentiment is healthy — and essential in the rocky, complex journey of learning to love yourself.

Your Baby

Imagine you have a baby. You love her with all your heart. You love her for exactly who she is, no matter what.

The fact that you love her implies you want to see her grow up healthy and strong.

You want her to learn and take responsibility.

You want her to be accountable and a good human being.

You want her to be independent.

What you want for this baby is the opposite of stagnation and conformity. There is disinterest in these things, desertion.

This objectively endearing, adorable baby is you. If you love and accept you just the way you are, you want to never stop becoming better. This is how loving yourself and wanting to improve can both be true.

Noticed

Forget about love.

Will I ever meet anyone?

Will I be noticed?

Set aside the questions and the wondering and the angst.

Instead, notice yourself. Who are you? Can you answer that?

What do you want? Are you sure?

Nobody is sure. We are certain we know what we want, but we don't.

What are your interests? Explore them. Be an explorer.

What are your projects? Make your life a quest and find them. Develop them. Bite off more than you can chew.

Exhaust yourself.

Who are your friends? Who do you consider family, blood related or otherwise? Be very interested in them. Spend time with them.

Read. Write. Travel. It doesn't have to be far. Wander down the streets of your neighborhood and look at things as if this place where you grew up was new, because it is.

Do all these things and watch them grow. Watch yourself become multidimensional. Watch the most beautiful thing — you, you as you unfurl.

Then, I promise. Everyone will notice.

How to Stop People Pleasing

Life is hard. Really hard. Finding my way takes grit and mostly means two things:

Making a distinction between what works for "everyone" and what works for me.

Finding the presence of mind to disappoint others in the name of standing up for myself.

People pleasing is disguised as generosity but really it's avoidance. It's constant, relentless escape from doing the hard work of not compromising myself.

The price is to not clearly understand who I am, to let people walk all over me, to feel full of bitterness and resentment and to wonder why I feel I am in the wrong life.

I am in the wrong life because if I people please I don't understand how to set boundaries and constantly allow others to make decisions for me.

Love yourself enough to know you are worth not betraying yourself in the name of getting others to approve of you.

A Practice

Loving yourself is not something you do but something you practice, a series of interconnected actions that involve treating yourself like something special and wonderful.

You eat well and exercise and do things to gently assist you in the battles that you fight — for example, I have anxiety and do my best to go to yoga, breathe, get a good night of sleep. I work hard at defying my own thoughts.

No, Dushka. What you worry about is not going to happen.

You step away from things that hurt you — friends who put you down or the job that doesn't fulfill or inspire you or the guy who, well, doesn't do what he says he's going to do.

You can do better, not because you can go find another man but because you have yourself.

You do things for you that you would do for someone you love — fun things like getting you those shoes you like and harder things like standing up for yourself, or following through on your own promises.

This is important because every time you do, you teach yourself you are worth trusting.

I can't go get drinks. I said I'd go to the gym four times a week and I skipped yesterday.

You do things that make you happy and let you get to know yourself and get really involved in creating something. A pie, a garden, a book. It doesn't matter what. It's yours and it's for you and maybe also supports others.

You take ownership of everything that affects your vital space — you build sacred things like habits and ceremony and boundaries. You come to terms with disappointing others. You learn to say no.

You say yes a lot too and surprise yourself by making unexpected plans — yes, yes. Book the trip to Japan. Get that beautiful painting so you can place it over your bed. Drink every day out of a beautiful faceted white cup.

Do senseless things, less for the objective and more for the sheer pleasure of it.

People who love themselves don't always. Loving yourself is like every other feeling — inconsistent, fluid, sometimes dismaying — but in the end you build a relationship with someone truly interesting you know you can count on.

Step by Step

Start with a cleanse.

Throw out the story of your life if you are not a hero in it. Buy a beautiful, brand new notebook. On the very first crisp, clean, blank page, write out your story. Take an objective look. Is it sad? Is it angry? Are you unlucky? Does it blame everyone else? Are you a victim? Do you have a sense of agency or do things seem to happen to you?

On the next page, change something. Own up to something. Be more accountable. Be more powerful. You have a whole notebook to page by page change your portrayal of the story of your life.

As the story in your notebook changes, notice the shifts in your real life.

Stop bad-mouthing you. Does your inner voice criticize you, put you down? Can you really work on something if your enemy is on the inside? If you are talking to yourself in a way that you would never speak to someone else, shut that shit down.

Don't spend any time with people who are not good for you. Is there anyone in your life constantly putting you down? Anyone you feel is toxic? Is anyone draining your energy? Do you have "frenemies" and can't explain why? You are fully responsible for the people you surround yourself with.

Stop comparing yourself to others. When you tell yourself someone has it better than you, you are never even getting the full picture. Focus on the work you have to do on yourself. Inside. Look inside. Inside is where it's at. Not outside.

Don't carry things that weigh you down. Are you feeling bitterness, anger, resentment, a drive for revenge? These things are the same as trying to get through a desert carrying poison instead of water. Throw it out. Let it go. Put it down. Forgive.

Forever give up on getting anything perfect. Instead, take risks. Do a terrible job and watch what happens. (I'll just tell you. Ready? Nothing. Nothing happens.) Every day, be absolutely relentless about learning something new.

Say no to things you don't want to do. This will often be met with disapproval. It might result in you losing some of those frenemies we talked about earlier. But, it will open up more time for you to do the things you need to.

There. Now that you have more time, more energy and a new perspective, here are some things to add to your life:

Nurture the glorious people who love you. Give them two things. Your time, and your full, complete attention.

Come into the fact that you're the boss. Forget about approval, what people will say or the fear of possibly making a mistake. (I'll just tell you. Ready? You will. You will definitely make a mistake.) What do you really want? What do you really want to do? Be your boss. You are your boss. Own up to it.

Make a list of things you are good at. In that same notebook that contains the evolving story of your life, make a list of things you are good at, or a list of things that fill you with pleasure. Do more of those things. They can make you feel competent (I'm a good listener!) or they can make you feel happy (I love walking barefoot in the grass!). Either way, discover, collect, list, repeat.

Make a list of things you find challenging. By "challenging" I don't mean "likely to cause you bodily harm". I mean things that make you uncomfortable that you know you need to do. Walk up and talk to a stranger. Ask someone out. Speak up. Develop opinions. Check off every single thing on your list. Start small. Start big. Either way, feel proud of all the times you did things you thought you couldn't do.

Learn to accept compliments. One of the great ironies of life is that it feels like criticism has a special, VIP pass right into our soul and compliments are not allowed in until they show ID and then upon inspection are asked to leave immediately. Let them in. Say thank you.

Take care of yourself. For me, this means eating better. Working at getting more sleep. Exercising regularly. Making a commitment to getting into shape does wonders for your self-esteem, teaches you about discipline, perseverance, dedication, and facing challenges. So much goodness rolled into a single objective.

Practice being a better person. Be kinder and more considerate. Do what you think is right. Every time I am mean, petty, cruel, dishonest, I suffer more than anyone. Other people get to walk away from me. I can't get away from myself.

Realize you have every kind of resource at your fingertips. If I am feeling blue, irritated, anxious, tired, I get help. I go to a yoga class. I read a book. I talk to someone I love. I find solace in the kindness of strangers. I go for a walk and make it a point to appreciate the color of the sky. I notice things around me that are there to support me if I fall.

I mean, even my seat cushion can be used as a flotation device.

Perfect Stranger

I am a stranger to myself.

I didn't know what I could do.

Or, to put it in clearer terms, there was a lot I was sure I couldn't do.

It seemed unfathomable.

It's possible there was an absence of self-esteem in the mix. But, honestly. Mostly it was a natural, healthy amount of general skepticism.

There were small things (the discipline of following through) and there were big things.

For example, college felt so overwhelming. *You are never going to finish, Dushka. You will never make it through the tangle of classes, never pass all these tests.*

And then I did.

And, who knows what you will do with your life. I can't see it. You will never find your way.

You will never be able to support yourself financially, seeing that all you want to do is write.

And then I did.

You will never survive divorce. How does one get through something like that, and start over, alone?

Watch me.

And, you will never get through your father's illness and death. How will you ever live in a world that doesn't have him in it?

Look. I'm still here.

You say you are going to write a book but how does one do that, actually write a book?

I went and wrote one. (And then another. Which was easier since now I knew I could.)

Now, after all the things I've done that I was absolutely certain I would be unable to do, I just wouldn't bet against myself.

It turns out that…well.

I believe in myself.

How can you believe in yourself? There is only one way.

Show you. Show you what you can do.

I can almost guarantee you'll be blown away by the incredible things this rather interesting person that you are can do.

Find Your Feet

As I get to know myself, as I find my feet, as I slowly learn how to establish my boundaries and protect them, I develop faith.

I don't mean in religion — I mean in myself.

This kind of faith is a powerful antidote to anxiety.

Faith in myself is how I come to trust that things will work out.

From this, I feel calmer. I suffer less.

I am less driven by what my ego wants me to do. I can soothe her when she freaks out, when she spins out, instead of mistaking her for me.

I realize nothing is personal and that people are doing the best they can so it becomes much easier to forgive and let go of what once would have hurt me.

My relationships are deeper, more meaningful, more deliberate, more peaceful. There is less drama, less entitlement, less blame.

I feel respected and valued because I respect and value myself.

I am more comfortable in the moment, this one right in front of me, because I can see my stories (both about the past and about the future) and can separate myself from them.

I enjoy the frankly delightful pleasure of my own company.

It is very, very powerful to learn to do for myself all the things I expected I could extract from others — approve of myself, validate myself, and be proud. Proud of myself.

Everything

There is no limit to how much I can change — for someone I love or for someone who doesn't matter.

I don't think I am always right, I don't believe everything I think and I am elastic, capable of a flip, a turn, a twist.

I change my mind, my opinion and my perspective. I back-pedal. I apologize.

Nothing about me is static. I love a new point of view and I love learning.

I grow. I evolve. I survive. I will surprise you. I will surprise myself.

Correct me. I already know I'm wrong.

Conversely, there is a lot I will not compromise — not for anyone. This is because I am solid.

You can count on me being who I am.

I am not and have never been impeccable, but I am reliable, dependable, predictable and stable.

All of these things are true in equal measure. I am not one thing or the other.

I am everything, and so are you.

Listen

Here are some examples of things I tell myself — except then I refuse to listen.

My body: *I'm tired.*

Me: *Wow. I don't know why I am so tired. Let me slug some coffee instead of resting.*

My body: *I need to pee.*

Me: *I think I'm just going to hold it in because I don't have time right now.*

My body: *I'm feeling sad.*

Me: *I'm sad. Instead of exploring why, let me find a distraction.*

My body: *This person is creepy.*

Me: *I don't know why I find this person creepy. Let me ignore my instinct and step into a small, soundproof, sealed metal box with them (also known as an elevator).*

My body: *This person is irritating me.*

Me: *I don't know why I find this person irritating. They are so nice. Why am I so difficult?*

My body: *I feel angry.*

Me: *Anger doesn't make sense right now. Shut that shit down.*

This is exactly like refusing to look at the compass in our pocket and lamenting that we feel lost.

We repeatedly silence our inner voice and then wonder why we can't find happiness.

The Best Shape for You

If you feel lost, like you don't know what to do with your life, like you have no idea what to do next, step one is to decide you are going to get in the best shape you have ever been in — the best shape for you.

Get up. Go on a run, or a walk, or a stretch. Join a gym, or a group. Just go.

In parallel, talk to a doctor. Do your research. How will you change your diet? What will you do for exercise? At what time? What works best for you?

In a life that feels rudderless, aimless, maybe even pointless, this alone will get you out of bed. It will give you structure, order and clear goals to move towards.

You will feel better as you get healthier. You will feel less blue, more motivated, more encouraged. You were designed to move.

As you get into your body you will tune into what you have been trying to tell you that you have been drowning out.

You will gain confidence as you begin to see the very real power you have to put yourself in a better place.

As one thing falls into place, other things will follow.

This is not easy. This is not instant. It's not magic. It's not linear. But it's real.

When you are lost, all you need is one small thing, an inkling, a hint, an intimation.

So, here. I will give it to you: it's your body.

The Mirror

Loving yourself means you are happy with who you see in the mirror. It's not that she's perfect. It's that it will always be OK that she never will be.

It means you are inside a virtuous circle of healthy choices. Not to look good to someone else. For you.

You recognize approval and praise feels delicious but are not your main source of motivation, inspiration or drive.

It means that you say goodbye to anything that isn't good for you. The person who plays games. The toxic friendship. The dead-end job. Your unsatisfactory living arrangements. Replays of the same argument. Things that should feed you but are somehow draining you.

It means going for the guy who shows up and follows through on what he says he's going to do.

It means you know you are enough and have enough. You stop doubting, second guessing, grasping.

It means you stop being suspicious and cagey and start feeling like others are doing their best. This is not about trusting everyone. It's about trusting yourself.

Your relationships might be flawed but are fundamentally healthy, easy, natural.

You realize that what other people want, prefer or reject is not related to you. Someone not being into you, for example, in no way implies you are less worthy of being loved.

You enjoy the frankly delightful pleasure of your own company.

You make time to pursue your interests, your projects and your creative endeavors.

It means you talk to yourself the way you'd talk to a loving friend, not your worst enemy.

Loving yourself means you steer clear of any activity you deem to be self-destructive.

It means you listen to yourself and give yourself what you need rather than trying to please someone else or struggling to be someone you are not.

You understand that if taking care of yourself is not your first priority you end up unable to take care of anyone else.

You don't gossip. You are too happy and busy with yourself to bother criticizing or complaining about others.

Other people's success makes you happy for them rather than angry, bitter, vengeful or vitriolic.

It means you are less afraid of making mistakes or taking risks because being bad at something doesn't result in you thinking less of yourself.

It means you regard yourself with clarity and accept you as you are, complete with unruly hair and impatient disposition.

It means you are always interested in improving and learning and understand that this point and the previous one will never be at odds.

Loud, Dirty Noise

Getting to know yourself is the key to happiness and is a process that will take the rest of your life.

You are living inside someone who will continue to surprise you.

This is because she's complicated, but mostly because she's not static.

You are attempting to get to know someone who is in a constant state of transformation.

If you want to get to know her, the first step is to make it a habit to spend time alone.

This is because above all else, we are chameleons. We are programmed to act like others, to belong, to fit in, to get others to like us.

We strive to "be normal", even if normal doesn't exist.

These desperate efforts to be like everyone else are the equivalent to loud, dirty noise over a clean, soft whisper.

Spending time alone allows you to hear yourself, to see what color you really are when you have nothing to blend into.

It helps too to resist putting yourself into slots. These are hard to defy because they are oversimplifications — they are easy, a fabrication of a lazy mind. They lack imagination.

Introvert or extrovert? A planner or spontaneous? You can be — and are — everything, often all at once. Dichotomies are not real. For true clarity, accept yourself as infinite and full of contradictions.

Finally, learn to distinguish fact from story. Most of what we find unsettling is just a story we have spun. It's the stories that make us suffer and blind us from seeing things as they are, including ourselves.

Truth Bullet

When I understood what I am about to tell you I felt I had been shot with a truth bullet.

Here it is: The best things in life happen without my intervention.

I don't need to do anything to be loved. I am loved because I am me and this requires neither action nor effort.

I don't need to be on my toes for someone not to cheat on me. I don't need to take care of him or keep him under constant surveillance.

Loyalty is the default and cheating the anomaly.

Betrayal is not supposed to happen and I don't need to do anything to ensure that this remains the case.

I don't have to convince, persuade or chase anyone or win anyone over to get or catch either a good friend or a significant other.

Love — in any iteration — is like gravity. I don't do anything to keep my feet firmly planted on the ground.

These things are so true that if I instead decide to act — to exert effort, to work at it, to aggressively pursue, to supervise everything — I attract unhealthy relationships and wonder where to cast the blame.

I walk away from any dynamic that requires me to compromise my peace of mind. I do less. A lot less. I do nothing and witness an upside down life right itself.

Well Adjusted

Loving yourself is synonymous with being well adjusted to the world.

It means that most of the time you believe you are enough and have enough.

Self-love allows you to love others, to be generous, to regard situations with compassion and to assume abundance.

Assuming abundance means I am secure enough to understand your success does not threaten or diminish me. You can do very, very well without having an impact on the fact I too can do well.

If you love yourself you have a clear sense of identity. You don't decide who to be or what to do based on what will get you the most approval or attention.

You allow others to see you for who you are.

This is because if you love yourself, you are less likely to perceive the world through your insecurities: you love who you are so don't compare yourself to others, don't worry others might suspect you are not good enough.

You treat others well, but also treat yourself well. You make healthy choices, recognize your efforts, and are secure enough to admire and look up to others.

You surround yourself with people better than you so you can always be learning.

By contrast, someone selfish cares only about herself. I make choices that are good for me, even if they are to the detriment of others. I operate under the belief I will not ever have enough and as such lack consideration for others.

I approach situations assuming scarcity — if you do well that means I will not do well.

Selfishness is a symptom of insecurity, a form of narrow-mindedness, an exhausting affliction of the soul. It's the very opposite of loving yourself.

Tinted Glasses

Every human, even a human who appears to be very confident, is in some measure insecure.

Being insecure is the emotional equivalent of putting on tinted glasses. It affects how I see everything.

If I am insecure, for example, I crave approval to the point of doing things in an effort to get more approval, rather than identifying and representing what matters most to me. This erases who I am.

How can I be loved, if I can't be seen?

If I am insecure, it's important that I get everything perfect. This means it's hard for me to admit I am wrong, to see another person's perspective, to be elastic, to try new things.

If I am insecure I am not sure that I am worth loving. I wonder if others are better than me. This leaves me open to jealousy, being possessive and territorial.

If I don't believe I am good enough I tend to look for people who agree. My insecurities in effect dictate who I find attractive.

I feel that nobody understands me, that nobody likes me, that I will always be alone.

Insecurity corrupts the intent and meaning of things, so I misunderstand everything, jump to the wrong conclusions, regard others with mistrust and suspicion.

I compare who I am, what I do and what I have with others and conclude everyone's life is better than mine. This breeds resentment, bitterness, envy.

By far the most difficult thing I have ever had to deal with in any relationship is me.

Look at That Kid

A dear friend of mine has a photo of herself as a kid on the wallpaper of her phone.

"This little girl," she says, *"was once innocent and perfect.*

"Maybe she grew up to make mistakes. Maybe she later did things that disappointed people. She possibly revealed herself as flawed. It's plausible that over the years she began to love herself less, to feel shame, to feel small, to self-sabotage.

"But that came later. Look at that kid."

When my friend needs to make a decision, she takes a good hard look at the photo on her phone. Because, it doesn't matter what came after. What matters is this: what is it that she wants for that little girl?

I look at a picture of me when I was four and conclude that the least I can do for her is everything.

My Projector

You carry the movie of you and a projector everywhere you go.

Then, you go to every single theater in your city, in the world, and wonder how it is that every place you go is showing the same film.

You realize that the images you see are not ever coming from the screen.

It looks like it's about the screen, but the source is your projector.

Our stories and insecurities have nothing to do with the outside world, nothing to do with our height or weight or looks or intelligence or aplomb or lack thereof.

They have to do with what we carry.

Resentment

Resentment is what I feel when I put someone's desires before my own in an effort to please or get another to think highly of me.

If the gesture comes from a place of generosity I feel happy, balanced.

If it comes from failing to represent myself I feel bitter and angry.

Resentment is a symptom of poor boundaries.

It comes disguised as me feeling anger towards another person, but I know better.

It's really me being angry at myself for not standing up for what I want, like, need or prefer.

It's what happens when I am not true to myself.

What If I Am Unattractive?

I am not going to tell you that beauty doesn't matter, or that it's a frivolous, empty attribute, because that is just not true.

I can instead offer something inarguable: that you can defy the definition of "attraction".

You have the power to be attractive for reasons other than looks.

You can work on developing a stunning intellect. You can be interesting and kind, compelling and compassionate.

Need I tell you how hot competence is? Learn to do things well.

People can be attracted to you for your strength, your vision, your capacity for attention, and a million other powerful, absolutely irresistible qualities.

You can be fascinating.

I can tell you other things about physical beauty that I know because I've felt them:

Beauty can be tiresome. *(Sure, you're good looking. But so what?)*

It's in the eye of the beholder, which means no one can compete with how beautiful you will look to someone who loves you.

It is as ephemeral as youth — maybe even more so.

What I'm suggesting instead has consequence, has influence, and has an everlasting potency.

And it's all right there, available to you.

Secret Ingredient

The secret ingredient of self-love is selflessness.

Love yourself. Know yourself. Own yourself. Respect your limits. Present your boundaries without compromise or apology.

Do all the giving, devoted things you would do for others for you.

The extra pillow, the soft blanket, the special meal, the silence and the space.

This way, you will always be ready to offer the most honest, the most integrated, the most well taken care of version of yourself to others.

Soul Mate

The greatest lie ever told is that there is someone out there who can make you peaceful, happy and whole.

If you suffer from a sense of dissatisfaction or despair, if you feel disheartened or lonely, it must be because you haven't found the person you are looking for.

This belief implants a permanent sense of restlessness.

What if instead I said you are already whole and that your secret sense of dissatisfaction and loneliness is inherent to the human condition?

No one out there has the ability to bail you out but you.

You can eventually pick someone to walk beside you to share in your experience, to rave about your good days and rant about your shitty days.

If instead of looking for a fix you run from person to person, you will run forever because the antidote to your emptiness does not exist in anyone outside of you.

Stop running. Give up that insatiable, desperate search. Love yourself. Know yourself. Save yourself. There is no one else.

Hold On to Who You Are

I love to write. I always have. And yet throughout my life my writing has been intermittent. It has never stopped but I have diminished it down to a trickle.

This is because I am an all-in sort of person, enthusiastic and extreme. When I enter a relationship I give it all I've got — my attention and my time. My intention and my energy. My focus and my determination.

I want to do things right.

Writing takes a lot. It is very time consuming and takes grit and discipline.

Oh, look. It takes the very same things a relationship requires.

So it was one or the other. *No, Dushka. You can't have both. You don't have the space, and you don't have the time.*

It took me decades to realize that what I was giving to my relationship was precisely what was killing it: I was suffocating it with my intensity and my vehemence.

And my writing? My writing was always there waiting for me. It did not ever require that I struggle to carefully modulate how much of me to give it. My writing could take me whole.

I don't know if losing yourself in a relationship is "normal". I've never been an authority on what that word actually means. I do know that it's common, and that it's a mistake.

You lose yourself willingly with the choices that you make, and one day the person your significant other fell in love with is no longer there.

So hold on to who you are — not in the name of selfishness but in the name of love. Not to be unavailable but to protect who you are, so you always have a lot of you to offer.

Because, if you are nowhere to be found, who is it that the other person is loving?

You've Changed

Do me a favor.

Step outside.

Look at the sky. Look at the clouds against it. Does anything remain static? Anything?

Look around. Look at grass, trees, streets, people. Notice how everything is in motion, a perpetual state of frenzied transformation.

Look inside you. Your moods, your feelings. Turmoil, yes? (Or maybe that's just me.)

Everything changes.

Do you know what the opposite of change is? Death.

Stagnation is the opposite of life.

It's what things do when they are done.

I change because I am alive. I change because I am not a rock. I am more like water. I change because I am a survivor.

There is someone dazzling inside you — someone you are going to become. Stop at nothing to be that person. Go back to who you were for no one.

The next time someone says you've changed, smile broadly and say thank you.

An Act of Insurgence

My brain is programmed to identify scarcity. This way, she thinks, I'm more likely to survive. So inside of me rings the angsty voice of my most primal self. *You are not enough*, she frets. *You don't have enough. You probably never will.*

And then, people. People and their opinions. People often make themselves feel big by making others feel small. Being judged and criticized is a relentless universal experience.

And my environment. Companies make money if I believe I need their stuff to make myself adequate. I will be fine but only with the right shoes and the right jeans and the right glow. If you buy this, buy into this, you will finally measure up.

Insecurity is big business.

But, you know what?

I love myself. I love myself just the way I am, and I think you should too.

Take that, world.

Hazy View

My hotel had a room with a splendid view.

I was in a gorgeous city on a beautiful day, but the windows were dirty.

Looking out was hazy, shadowy, dim, blurry.

With a transparent window, the view would have been definite, lucid, sheer.

You can love someone when you don't love yourself. But your view will not be clear.

Things to Keep in Mind Before Starting a Relationship

Ready — Not Ready

Signs that I am ready for a relationship:

I am in no rush.

I thoroughly enjoy my own company and the chance to be alone.

I have my own interests and pursuits.

My life feels purposeful.

I am aware of my patterns and can recognize them when they present themselves.

I understand that just because I feel something doesn't mean I have to act on it.

I don't expect another person can possibly make me happy, fulfilled or whole.

Signs that I'm trying to fill a void:

I'm lonely.

I don't want to be alone.

Whenever I am in a relationship I seem to fight and break up for the same reasons. *I am so unlucky in love. Where are all the good guys? Where?*

I have not met you but already love who I imagine you to be.

As soon as I find my other half I will be happy and my life will fall into place.

As soon as I find my soul mate his interests and pursuits will be my interests and pursuits.

My one and only will magically meet my expectations of love.

Unrequited Love

When I am in love with someone who doesn't love me back I don't fix it by not loving him.

I mean, don't get me wrong — I try to. I try not to love him.

But my heart is this wild, sovereign, beating thing that never listens to me.

What I do instead is make peace with this love. The love will have to stay.

I love him, but also I deserve more than someone who doesn't love me.

Spending every day with him, hanging out with him, having him in my space, in my house — no.

I'm hurting myself with this choice that I keep making, and it's been long enough.

I might not be able to stop loving him, but you know what I can do? I can stop giving him my time, and I can stop giving him my space.

I give these things to myself instead, time alone, the chance to learn new things, spend time with people who appreciate and love me.

Eventually, slowly, the love begins to dwindle, because I'm not feeding it with the frantic hope, and his daily presence.

It's not easy to say no and walk away and do other things.
It's not easy but I have to because even if he does not love me, I love me.

And I am the one who keeps doing this to myself.

One more thing. I never, ever tell myself that I don't have the strength to do something. I have the strength to do anything.

This is because strength does not come from declaring its lack of existence.

It's strength that begets strength, and it's this that has proven to me I can do anything.

I can do anything, and so can you.

Don't Settle

You are responsible for your happiness. It's something you give yourself — not something another can take responsibility for.

Settling is not really related to what others do or don't do for you.

Settling means deciding that less of what you really want will be enough. It means making a decision that short-changes you. Deciding to settle is usually driven by fear.

It sounds like this:

I don't really love him, but I'm going to marry him because I don't want to end up alone.

This is not really what I want to do with my life, but I don't know what I really want to do so I'm just going to go with this.

I have already spent so much of my time at this job. I don't like it, but I don't want what I've already done to go to waste.

Your life is the sum of your decisions. If you settle, it stands to reason that the life you end up with will fall short when you compare it to the life you really want.

What If He Doesn't Text Me Back?

Put the phone down. Step outside. Go for a stroll. Look at beautiful things.

Make arrangements to see someone you love who you haven't seen in a while. Catch up.

Buy flowers and place them somewhere where you can see them. Buy flowers and take them to someone else, maybe someone who could use a splash of color in their life.

Go to a bookstore and browse and make a list of all the books you want to read. Discover some new interest. You've never been a gardener. Why are so many of the books you are picking up about gardening? Explore that.

In that same bookstore go to the travel section and make a list of three places you want to visit. They don't have to be far.

Catch a movie. Fly a kite. Go for a run. Attend an exercise class. Enroll in a dance class, maybe tango. Whoa. It's so sexy.

Get a haircut. Get a facial. Get a massage. Go to a restaurant and taste something new.

Take stock of your life. What are you happy with? What are you not happy with? Make a change. It can be tiny. It can be huge.

Surprise yourself. You never, ever get tea. Who is this person inside you, this tea drinker? Get to know her. She will always be a mystery to you. I know this because whenever I pay attention I realize I am a mystery to myself.

I like her, this multifaceted stranger that lives inside of me.

At some point, in an hour or a day, he might text you back.

You will have so much to tell him.

And, if he doesn't, well. You have so much to do.

Are Flowers Weird on a First Date?

Tell me.

Is taking flowers to a first date something you would like to do?

I am asking because many, many women would find it weird.

But many others (like for example me) would find it super thoughtful and sweet.

And, you know what dates are for?

The purpose of a date is to determine compatibility.

If you would like to bring flowers and find the woman expressing discomfort, then you have your first sign that this person might not be for you.

If the woman instead is touched and expresses gratitude, you are a step closer to finding someone who likes you for exactly who you are.

This is what people mean when they say "be yourself".

Friends With Benefits

I used to think "friends with benefits" was what you called someone you just didn't love. Sure, there was chemistry and therefore sex, but this person could not be "upgraded" to you (or him) calling it a relationship.

Now I realize the colossal power of the word "friend". Friends are there for you. They are interested in your endeavors, and you in theirs. You come through for each other.

Friendships frequently outlast most relationships by years, even decades.

Relationships have a tangle of binds. They have more burdens, more expectations and more demands. Being fully compatible is a requirement if you are to have a harmonious life.

Friends love you the way you are, roll with your quirks and idiosyncrasies instead of wanting you to change them.

A lack of compatibility is less of an issue as this type of relationship comes with more room.

You most definitely love a friend with benefits — and can, of course, fall in love. This is because even when we decide and agree to "not fall for each other", we don't govern our hearts.

But, in friends with benefits, the dynamic between the two of you has room to ebb and flow. You can love and not, fall in and out of love, and witness the rock solid foundation of who you are — the friends part — hold you together much better than a significant other surviving you don't love them anymore.

Boundaries

A personal boundary establishes where you end and another person begins. It's about limits, and how far you are willing to go.

Knowing where your boundaries are is key to healthy relationships.

Some examples might be:

I love you, but sometimes I need to be alone. This does not mean I don't want to be with you.

I love you but sometimes I will say no to you.

I love you, but sometimes I want to spend time with my friends. This does not mean I am choosing them over you.

You cannot choose my friends for me.

When we have sex, I like that, that and that, but I don't want to do that. "No" is enough — I don't need to explain why.

I need to be treated with love and with respect. I am not OK with you being critical or harsh, even if you think you are doing it for my own good. I am not OK with low blows when we fight.

I am a private person. You cannot look through my things or open my phone. This does not mean I am hiding something.

Boundaries are fluid. What is comfortable for you one day can be something you don't want to do the next day. Boundaries require clear communication.

I'll Never Find Love

My friend assures me she will never, ever find love so what's the point?

What is the point of trying, of going out, of setting up dates? Why, if she already knows she is unlovable?

This is a delusion, of course. Something that is not necessarily true that she has chosen to believe.

The reason why it's important to become aware of things you choose to believe is that you have the power to create your reality.

This is called a self-fulfilling prophecy: the ability to make real the things you fear the most.

Better Than a Fairy Tale

When I was young, I bought into the preposterous, pop culture, pink bubble gum, fairy tale notion of a "soul mate". My other half. My perfect fit missing piece.

I have confirmed there is no such thing. As it turns out, this is excellent news, because reality is better than any fairy tale.

Here it is: I was created whole, spectacularly whole, and am in effect my own perfect missing piece.

I am the one in possession of the answers to all my questions, which works supremely well as I can always make me totally available to myself.

In addition to me, I have at my disposition the vast richness and delight I find in other people and in all the things they make me feel.

I have a very broad, very wide list of things I need, want and enjoy, and a very broad, very wide list of places I can find it.

A friend I can sit in silence with. A friend who makes me think. A friend who makes me laugh. A friend who makes me feel fortunate or grateful. A friend who keeps my secrets. A friend I feel absolutely safe with. A new friend with a fresh perspective. A friend who has known me forever.

For example, my friend Carla, who I met the very first day I went to college. I have had hundreds of friends since then, many deep and glorious and meaningful.

Still, no one has ever threatened her special place in my heart.

Every relationship I establish is different, and as such each one has its own sovereign space that cannot possibly be infringed upon by another.

I am unable to find everything I need in a single person. But, why would I want to? Why would I deny the very best part of life, which is what other human beings (and other creatures, such as puppies or even flowers) are able to offer us?

This is like attending a buffet and arbitrarily deciding that all you can eat are the poached eggs.

Poached eggs are delicious, with their runny, eggy, yolky goodness, but look at the bounty spread across dozens of tables. Why would you decide to turn your back on everything in exchange for just one thing?

If I allow my insecurities to rule my life then I want to own people and be all they have and all they need and all they want.

The problem is this is not real, it is not true, it is not possible and it is not healthy.

Instead, I work on believing in myself and in the connections that I make.

I believe that, just like anyone I have a relationship with cannot find everything he needs in me, he also cannot find anywhere what he finds in me.

Instead of squeezing your fists in fear and despair and agony and saying "mine, mine, mine" when you love, open your mind. Open your heart. Open your hands — wide, wide open.

Leap. Trust yourself.

Whisper these words whenever you need to, the most beautiful, the most healthy words:

Everything I love is free.

Go. Go find whatever it is that you need.

I will be here when what you need is what you find in me.

Attached

I think it was the way he smelled.

I wondered about it, and then it was nothing like all that wondering.

It was better. So much better.

Or his texture. I have a thing for texture and he was so soft.

I like running my hands across and along soft things and I suspect he was specially designed.

Or the fact I didn't really know him at all. It's not so much that he was a mystery but rather that he was exotic.

Like how is it possible that you could even exist out here, outside the confines of my imagination?

Or the fact that I knew all along getting attached was off limits and my heart is insubordinate at best.

Or that most of the time when I wanted to talk he agreed to but would say nothing at all.

It made me wonder — me, a writer, a language lover — if what the whole world needs is less words, rather than more.

We get attached for every reason.

We get attached for no reason.

Is There a Crush You Regret?

A crush is sensation, a feeling, overwhelming, all absorbing — you. All I want is you.

I do not determine my feelings. They spring up involuntarily, spontaneously, surprise me with their force and their ferocity.

If I decide this crush gets to dictate my actions, I might or might not feel remorse over what I decide to do.

But a crush on its own is not something I can feel contrite about.

I cannot regret what I have no control over.

Lies Are Not the Way

Some people are monogamous and some are not.

If I believe monogamy is The Way and am not monogamous, I feel I have only one choice to make room for who I am: I lie. I cheat. I say *"you are my one and only"* and *"I only have eyes for you"* and I go establish relationships with others and justify this by calling them "casual".

I insist *"they don't mean anything"* except I have less control over my feelings than I thought and sometimes they do. They do mean something. If not to me, then to the person I thought I was having a fling with.

Nothing is working. Everything is catching up to me. What a mess.

One day I have an epiphany: holy shit. What people have been saying to me about life does not work for me.

There has to be another way because this is exhausting. I want to stop it with the lies.

I start telling the truth and it's hard and it's painful because people who wanted the person I was pretending to be fall away.

But others stay.

Telling the truth is the most worthwhile filter. It selects the people who love me for who I am.

My lifestyle becomes possible and this does not save me from catastrophes but it saves me from having to cheat and lie and hide who I am.

Of course, I am using monogamy as a metaphor. This is about being who I am. Identifying what that is in the middle of a cacophony of conflicting voices and deciding to be that and refusing to hide.

It's about resolving not to lie as a way of life, in particular not lie precisely to the people who love me.

Find who you are. Be true to that. If one day you realize your choices demand that you lie to everyone know this: mostly you are lying to yourself.

Compatibility

Compatibility refers to an ability to exist with someone else with a minimal amount of friction.

This sounds simple, but is tangled up in all sorts of complexity.

This complexity has less to do with getting to know another person and more to do with recognizing that the problem here is me.

I see what I want to see. Which means that if I decide I like you and you behave in ways that are not compatible with me and I am in the throes of the fog of infatuation, our incompatibility will be camouflaged to the point of making invisible something that is right in front of me.

To put it in other words, the chemical cocktail flooding my bloodstream will blind me to the fact that we both know there is no alternate universe where this can possibly end well.

I am under the impression that love conquers all and am open and willing to change something in me that is fundamental. (Let me tell you how this ends: I can't. I can't change something in me that is fundamental.) The truth is love does not conquer all. A lack of compatibility will sooner or later eat love for breakfast and spit out the bones.

I am convinced I can change the other person. He is super messy and I am neat and with our hearts filled to the brim with love I will gently guide him every day towards the glory that is picking up his shoes. Let me save you years of effort, time and despair: you cannot change another person. You cannot change another person. You can't, and you need all that time and effort to work on yourself.

I am not a rock. I am water. I know you've probably heard the saying "people don't change" but the fact is we do. We change a lot.

I can come into a relationship firmly believing I want certain things and then having a change of heart. I don't want to break the promises I made, but that big, existence-altering thing we agreed was important to both of us? I don't want it anymore, and now, keeping that promise implies completely ruining the only life I get. What then?

If we are in a constant state of flux, can we ever really get to know another person?

Clearly, the solution here is to avoid attachment until we get all this sorted out.

Except, avoiding attachment can't be done. I get attached all the time to people I have no business being attached to.

Oh, heart. Not again.

NO HEART THIS MAKES NO SENSE

While this instant attachment I am afflicted with has the potential to make me suffer, I also believe it's a big part of the reason why I am such a happy person. Crushes fill me with a life-affirming electric current of joy. They inspire me, make me more creative and aware.

A crush brings out the best in me, and it's up to me to keep it circling through me rather than expecting a forever and ever with the unsuspecting guy who probably didn't even notice how that thing he did when he scrunched his shoulders in felt like someone shot an arrow through my heart.

I am a human, and was created to feel. This is a privilege and not something I ever want to be protected from.

Good Dates

I once told a guy I loved fresh flowers and on a date we sauntered through a large flower market.

I met someone else over dinner with friends and everyone was talking about a movie I hadn't seen. He asked if I wanted to watch it with him.

Normally a movie date is not ideal if you want to get to know someone but in this case it was so appropriate to the conversation we had met over. It also gave us something specific and easy to talk about over a meal afterwards.

I've gone on first dates to bookstores where we show each other books we have liked, then each recommend and maybe buy a book the other would enjoy. Boyfriend and I still do this even after years of living together.

Strolling through a museum can be fun too, picking an interesting exhibit and noticing what catches the attention of the other. Many museums have really nice coffee shops which make extending the date quite natural.

On a date once we went to a dog park expressly to be dog observers. We alternated walking and sitting on benches in the sun.

The best dates are not generic but personal, related to something the other person has revealed interests them.

Plus the fact that you were paying attention says a lot about you.

How to Get Him to Love You

I have the answer and I am going to give it to you but it's going to take you many years to believe me.

You can be a disaster, a catastrophic girlfriend, and have a man eating out of the palm of your hand, entranced, unable to stay away.

You can be perfect, a dream, the girlfriend he — not everyone, but he specifically — has always wanted, and lose him anyway.

The only thing to do here is be as true to yourself as you can.

Understand your own boundaries and set them down clearly. Get to know yourself, which is so much harder than it seems.

Love yourself and treat yourself kindly and find ways to stretch and improve and nourish this person you are discovering.

Create habits and set goals and dedicate yourself to them.

Take responsibility, pursue your interests and get to know the world around you.

Find yourself. Find yourself. Everything comes and goes. The guy will love you, or he won't. But this way, you will always have you.

Now for the final twist — it's precisely this self-possession that makes someone hard to resist.

Can Flirting Be Taught?

Flirting is flair, part personality, part technique.

There are many, many different ways to flirt.

You can be subtle or direct, funny or serious, wanton or reserved, outrageous or clean, hesitant, sure, merciless, cautious, wayward, capricious, playful, deliberate, arbitrary, systematic, controlled, planned, goalless, accidental, undirected, purposeful.

In my opinion, flirting can be taught as long as the technique is consistent with the rest of the student's personality.

A very, very reserved person might (for example) come across stilted if she tries to flirt very directly or aggressively but might do well if she finds her own more nuanced style.

In short, you might not be able to flirt like your super flirtatious friend, but you can flirt like you.

I Can't Be That

Sometimes I feel that no matter what I do I can't be the person someone else wants me to be.

I don't conclude I am wrong for that person. What I arrive at is that there is something wrong with me.

Feeling that there is something wrong with me is an infallible indication that I need a "time out".

I need to hang out with me for a while.

I need to take his demands and reactions out of the equation.

During this time with me, I ask myself the following questions:

"Who am I?" — rather than *"How can I be what he wants me to be?"*

"What is it that I want?" — rather than *"How can I guess what he wants so I can give him that?"*

"What is right for me?" — rather than *"What is right for him and how can that be me?"*

Being who I really am is the only person I can always be.

Trying to be just right for someone else compromises me, for two reasons: because despite my efforts I can't ever get it right, and because it's not something I can sustain.

Being who someone else demands is not something I can consistently do without becoming intensely frustrated, confused and resentful.

I come out of my "time out" and lovingly, expansively say *"Here you go. This is me".*

If "this is me" feels wrong to the other person (for example: "normal" to me, "smothering" to him) then I conclude we are not right for each other.

This might be frightening and painful, but much less so than a lifetime of feeling that there is something wrong with who I am.

Should I Tell Him How I Feel?

I tell the people that I love how I feel.

I blurt it out *oh wow I love you* even when I probably shouldn't, even though it's not time yet, you know, *too early*, even though *Dushka, my god love is a big word* or *don't you think this is dangerous?*

You know what's dangerous? The times I said nothing, kept it to myself. Because how terrifying. Because what if they freaked out, left, thought I was weird, couldn't handle it, couldn't handle me?

What if I am too much?

Let me tell you, the times that I said it felt like release, like a huge exhale, like *here take this, I want you to have it. You don't have to do anything with it and neither do I but look, how beautiful.*

The times I said nothing this magnolia love, fresh, substantial, generous, became a diminished dark thing coiled around my esophagus. Something heavy and unwieldy I had to drag around and hide.

Then it just hung there between us like a lie, like dead weight, like a burden, like something nobody wanted instead of what love is supposed to be: coveted, wide, winged, a privilege, sublime.

Mix It Into Everything

My heart is a lot like my hair.

She's lawless and willful and does her thing no matter how much I try to contain her.

When I love someone I shouldn't, or someone who doesn't love me back, I take that unruly love and sneak it into various, much needed, maybe forsaken places.

I put it to use, rather than lugging around something this unwieldy.

That extra squeeze in the snuggly hug I gave my lonely friend was all for her, but also it was for you.

The added effort in my backbend in yoga was all for me, but also it was for you.

The enthusiasm displayed in the early morning meeting was for that team, and yeah. It was for you.

And then there's the flowers. The flowers I post on Instagram (look at those yellow roses with their snazzy design) are for anyone who goes there looking for something in what I write — but also, they are for you.

I would send you flowers if I could. Not on Valentine's Day, because ugh to saccharine holidays, but every day.

Flowers on the bed, for you.

And for everyone else — do you carry around love you have nowhere to put?

Mix it into everything.

In one form or another it will come back to you. Just you wait and see.

Meant to Be

There is no "meant to".

How long my relationships last is not determined by a mysterious force busy writing stories about my fate.

I meet someone and I decide if I want them in my life for the short term or the long term.

What happens next depends entirely on our investment in each other, on the decisions that we make, on the work that we put in, on how we choose to handle adversity and where we choose to focus our attention.

There is no relationship that is "meant to be", and no relationship that dwindles because "it was not meant to be".

You will it to be, or you don't.

I'm in Love With My Friend

Crap.

So you have feelings for your friend.

Let me start by telling you what has never worked for me:

"Oh no. I think I have feelings for him. This will ruin our friendship and therefore I will keep my feelings a secret."

This flawed logic makes everything strange because I begin to react to things he cannot see.

To my feelings, I am being consistent. To him, I am acting deranged.

As such, the first step is to accept: This is a calamity. There is nothing I can do. I don't choose how to feel and if I am feeling this way, this friendship will already be in for a whole lot of change.

To make this as not weird as possible I deliberately decide to be clear, direct, the opposite of coy. I don't speculate, guess or try to "read the signs."

This is an exhausting recipe for a roller coaster of emotions — *OMG HE FEELS IT TOO* — *No! No! He feels nothing this is devastating!* — *OH MY GOD HE ADDED AN EXTRA SQUEEZE TO OUR HUG!!!*

So, I just tell him.

This can be awkward as hell but face it, Dushka. It already is.

"I am going to tell you something that might make things awkward between us for a while so let's promise each other to let it be awkward and work through this together, ok?

"I have feelings for you. If you don't feel this too, just be patient with me until I work this out. I just wanted to give you visibility into what I'm going through."

After this I might decide I need a few weeks to myself just so I'm not seeing him every day.

Hopefully the long term result is that we are solid friends and this is just one more thing our resilient friendship has gone through.

Or, it turns out that extra squeeze did indeed mean he feels the same way, in which case we get to begin a new phase in our relationship.

Love/Addiction

You meet someone and oh my god he seems perfect. (I don't mean to crush you with this terrible news but this sensation is temporary. Because, you know, right? Nobody is perfect.)

But there you are in the phase of love where you are convinced of this perfection.

You love what this person can give you.

And, you just can't wait to see him again — and he can't wait to see you again.

There is a rhythm, a cadence, that suggests you are both in the same intoxicating place.

You talk about the future. Maybe not about "forever" quite yet but *"we can watch that other movie next weekend"* and *"some day we will go to Spain because my best friend lives there and I can't wait to introduce you"*.

You like each other and get each other and he smells good and yep. You are falling in love.

Or.

You meet someone and oh my god he seems perfect. And, this sensation is not temporary because it just feels like no matter what happens, you can't seem to get out of it.

You want with all your being all the things this person will never be able to give you.

You feel a gaping hole: like you just can't get enough. It doesn't matter how often he texts or calls or how often you see him you want more. More.

It's you who is texting and chasing. This is not balanced. This is not mutual. This is you. And you don't understand exactly what it is you're chasing if it's quite clear there is nowhere to go from here. There is no future here.

And, I mean, am I even lovable? Am I even worth anything? Why is this so incredibly painful? Why do I feel like I want to die? Yep. This is addiction.

No Strategy

I have no idea how to "keep a man interested".

This is because the act of keeping a man interested implies a strategy and requires that I play a certain role.

Play hard to get, maybe. Pretend I'm less interested than I am. Try to be cool. Be eager, but not needy. Text less. (Or is it more?)

The problem is that I am super chatty. Naturally enthusiastic. On a scale of 1 to 10, I am geeky: 10, cool: zero. I'm intense, quirky as all hell, and frequently claim to be dangerously snuggle deprived.

All this to tell you that anything that requires I play any role is not really who I am and as such is not something I can sustain. Bits of truth will leak out at inopportune moments.

For example, I have a tendency to stare adoringly at the guy I'm into.

Sooner or later (sooner, really) he will realize I am not what I represented myself to be. (Tragically, the aloof, mellow and standoffish look is just not credible on me.)

The only long term strategy that I have found effective is to immediately be everything I am. Speak up for what I think, like and believe in. Request outright the snuggling I require.

If a guy likes these things he will stick around. If he doesn't, he wasn't going to anyway, and why on earth would I want a guy who doesn't want me for the things I am?

Immediately displaying everything I am efficiently eliminates all the people I really shouldn't be spending any time on.

Why Did He Stop Texting?

If a guy told me I was attractive and then failed to text me I would wonder what the heck happened.

Then I would remember that when people do or don't do things, my existence is not the only variable.

It's possible that him texting or not texting has nothing to do with me.

For example:

    He has a lot of work

    He lost his phone

    He is spending time with friends

    He is spending time with family

    He is trapped under something heavy

    He doesn't usually text

It helps me put things in perspective, to keep in mind I am not at the center of any of the things that happen around me.

What Should a First Date Be Like?

On a first date you can look at each other from across the table and talk.

You can decide to not even bother with ordering dinner and go straight to your place, or his.

Your date can include or not include breakfast. (Maybe just coffee, so you can make a mental note of how he takes it.)

On a first date you can go for a walk and keep your distance, or hold hands or hook arms.

You can decide you want no contact, or go to a park and lie on the grass side by side and see how the whole length of his body feels against yours.

You can wave goodbye from three steps away or embrace and find — wow. He feels good against me.

There is no "should". It's your date. You get to decide.

Signs of Control

You are mine.

You belong to me.

I don't like your friends.

I don't think you should hang out with ____. He's bad news.

You spend too much time on the phone with your sister.

I think you should stop eating sweets/wearing short dresses/coloring your hair.

I criticize you, but it's for your own good.

You'd look better in high heels/with straight hair/with tighter clothes/if you used makeup.

You would if you loved me.

I would do it for you.

I do a lot more for you than you do for me.

I can't believe you would do that to me.

You owe me.

I need to look at your phone.

I need all your passwords.

If you're doing nothing wrong, this should not be a problem.

I can't stand it when someone else looks at you.

I can't stand it when you look at someone else.

I don't understand why you'd need time alone.

You're not working late. You are cheating on me.

I was just teasing you.

You're not as good as you think you are.

If you ever leave me I will kill myself.

If you ever leave me I will kill you.

Love Doesn't Hurt

We feel many things that we confuse with love.

We feel the need to control and feel frustration when we realize we don't own another person.

We feel anger when we realize we are powerless when it comes to trying to change someone else.

We feel expectations, when we want the other person to do what we'd like, and disappointment when they don't.

We feel guilt, when these expectations are turned back on ourselves and we feel we are supposed to do or be something.

We feel insecurity when we realize love does not come with any guarantee.

We feel the twisted consequences of these things in the form of jealousy, envy, anger, doubt, inadequacy.

All these things hurt like the fires of hell but these things aren't love.

Love is the ability to clearly see someone for who they are and to want what is best for him, whatever makes him happy. It feels expansive — the opposite of miserable.

A Completely Inappropriate Crush

Oh my god that's crazy. Oh my god that's thrilling. Oh my god the agony.

What a delicious, spectacular catastrophe.

Look, my heart is a calamity. I develop crushes regularly and always considered a crush was a demand, a command — *Dushka, do something!* — but I have learned it's less about doing and more about feeling, feeling in all its madness, incongruence, intensity, wonder and pain.

Feeling like this — ah, yes, this! — reminds me of everything I want: this crackle instead of the meh.

It's like I'm young again.

A crush is to me an indicator that it's time to ask myself a lot of questions and take stock of the life I have that I can suddenly regard in a clear, new light.

Why? Why do I feel like this? What is it in my life that I have grown complacent with, and how did I get here?

What in me needs to be resuscitated with a jolt of electricity?

Is it my relationship? My job? Is it me, is it my days, safe, uniform and predictable?

And why is there nothing alarmingly sexy in my closet? Where did that go, and when, exactly?

I need to shock something, overturn something, disturb something. Something here needs attention. Something has to change.

A crush is for me a reckoning.

My hope is that with this kind of analysis I can both welcome and make room for this blaze of feelings while gently putting things back where they belong. Without burning down anything valuable, without betraying or hurting someone important and without doing something I can never take back.

It's hard, so hard, like taming lightning.

But just because I feel something doesn't mean my life has to be doused in gasoline.

I Kissed My Friend

He was my best friend. I kissed him.

Or wait. I think he kissed me.

No. He definitely kissed me.

Once we'd committed this gigantic transgression we were both like *"well, we've already done this"* so kissed again. It ended up being an evening of kissing.

It was so fun.

It was a catastrophe.

We told each other nothing would change and then kissed some more. You know. To say goodnight.

The next day instead of calling him like I usually did I waited for him to call me.

And instead of calling me first thing like he usually did, he didn't call.

This was off to a terrible start.

Late that evening I called him. *"Dude. We're off to a terrible start."*

We talked and talked. We hung out the next day and talked some more.

All this talking was somewhat helpful but not really.

You know what helped? Accepting that for a while things were going to be super awkward and being willing to just feel awkward and hang out anyway.

To consider our relationship valuable enough to stick it out and push through as much awkwardness as would be necessary.

Eventually things went back to normal.

What Do You Want?

Trying to be friends with someone I am in love with is really hard.

It can be incredibly painful, and there is no official recipe for it: the "right or wrong way" is up to me.

What has helped me is to clearly determine what I want.

Am I only interested in him romantically?

Am I pretending to be his friend in an effort to get him interested? (This does not work and disregards what he wants from me.)

Or does the fact that I want him in my life mean more to me than how he is in my life?

If this is the priority, to make sure he is in my life because I find him valuable, I recognize that the pain I am feeling, as awful as it is, is temporary — and the friendship, his inclusion in my life — is the long game.

I remind myself I am playing the long game.

Should I Marry Him?

I don't know. I don't know if you should marry him.

Instead, I can tell you I look very closely at who I surround myself with.

So much of my life and who I become is determined by my relationships — all of them: coworkers, friends, significant others.

I have learned that relationships should free me. By this I mean they should inspire me, nurture me, encourage me, support me, help me grow, open me up, make me better.

They should contribute to me amassing a large collection of people who love me.

They are not supposed to control me, limit me, suffocate me, trap me, put me down, isolate me, keep me from what I love, turn life into a constant, exhausting negotiation where it becomes increasingly difficult to find a sliver of happiness.

This is as far as I can go, because who you decide to marry is up to only one person, and that is you.

How to Ask Her Out

"Dushka," my mom yells. *"Can you come upstairs? You have a delivery."*

Plopped in the middle of the living room sat a gigantic box.

I stared.

"What is it?" says my mom.

"Mom. I have no idea. I just got here."

"Who sent it?"

I look at her.

I walk over to the box. I circle it. I try to tip it. I expect 3 people to jump out (that's how big it is) and am surprised to discover it's light.

We stand there.

I go get a knife. I gently cut the box open. Balloons fly out and bump against the ceiling.

One of them has an invitation tied to the string.

Let's go out on a date! the card says. *Signed, Randall.*

"Who is Randall?"

Randall was a guy I barely registered. I met him at the school library and we waved. From afar. The next day I ran into him again and he introduced himself. That was it. I did not know how he got my address.

I was kind of sort of mildly flattered, but mostly it was excessive and a bit out of place. I felt uncomfortable.

I know that in movies grand gestures are made and people swoon and love ensues indefinitely.

But in real life grand gestures are — weird. Invasive. Sometimes creepy.

Believe me when I tell you that the best way to ask someone out is *"Hey. Let's go out! What sounds good? Coffee? Tea? A walk?".*

If she wants to go out with you, she will be thrilled. Not because you're dazzling. Just because you're you.

Will I Ever Find Perfect Love?

If I state that I want to find someone perfect what I am really saying is that I'm unavailable.

Looking for someone perfect means I will be furiously looking, leaving no stone unturned, giving the impression to others and to myself that I am trying, trying, yet coming up with nothing.

This is how I can refrain from ever admitting the truth: that I am not ready for a relationship.

More to the point, finding someone perfect would demand that I be perfect myself. I'd have to begin by finding a way to erase my rocky relationship history, the fact that I find relationships the most difficult thing.

I'd have to learn how to become a better listener and how to be interested in everything my partner talks about, including the model of cars that he likes (and why) and his long, winding story about that package that was never delivered.

I'd have to figure out how to sustain my adolescent ardor past the beginning of the relationship.

I'd have to make my own coffee instead of feeling the delight I feel in someone making it for me.

Oh no. I would probably have to learn how to cook.

I'd have to make certain that none of the things I do are done in an attempt to control or manipulate. I would never, not once, be able to frown or pout or glare.

I'd have to be steady, predictable and unfailingly kind instead of moody and mercurial. I'd have to find a hiding place big enough to stuff my frequent exasperation.

I don't know. I don't know if I could find a way to be tolerable 100% of the time.

The only thing I can guarantee 100% is that I am going to hurt you. And not be who you need me to be. And disappoint you. And not meet your expectations.

Not because I'm flawed (because I am). But because if you are expecting to find someone perfect you are destined, beyond not finding what you are looking for, to a life of pain and disenchantment.

Better to learn how to be exactly who I am and accept the same in others.

There's No Rush

Before I ever had sex I engaged in intense, electrifying make out sessions that were so much fun.

Sex is magnificent but I sometimes wish I could go back to making out the way I used to, in that thrilling, disordered, uninformed fashion that cannot be replicated once you've gone all the way.

Marriage is similar. Being married is splendid but once you are married you can't go back to being single, back to having all that space and angst and doubt and longing.

I look back and wonder why on earth I was always in so much of a rush.

Relish what you have. Delight in whatever now is, all the glory and discomfort.

It will all come soon enough and then you'll know for certain that you always made the best of whatever it was that presented itself.

The Rules

The most common mistake we make when we date is the assumption that we need to "catch up" on the rules we are supposed to follow.

How are things done these days? What is it that I need to do to conform, fit in to this mysterious new dynamic?

We have it backwards. The rules are not set for us to follow.

Instead, we are the designers of these rules, the architects, and what we decide to do determines who we attract.

Take the three day rule: if I go out on a date and really like him, I am supposed to wait three days before contacting him again, lest I come across as too eager.

But, if I wait three days I begin to attract people who think this preposterous and arbitrary rule is worth following.

Instead, I want a man who can think for himself.

A clear communicator with the courage to tell me he likes me, one willing to show enthusiasm for me and the time we spent together.

"Before we go our separate ways I want to tell you I had a lot of fun and would love to see you again. Does Thursday work for you?"

This criteria puts both of us above "the game." I set the rules and pay no mind to "how things are done", and am looking for the kind of person who agrees.

Things to Know Before You Get Married

You don't really understand yourself.

You don't really know what you want.

You don't really understand another or know what they want.

Your emotional baggage prevents you from seeing things clearly.

Your feelings are not like roots, stable and steady. They are like a storm, unsettled, unpredictable, turbulent. Or maybe that's just me.

You can't delegate happiness.

Loneliness is not the absence of others. It's something inside and nothing outside can mend it.

Marriage does not protect you from your internal appetites and as such cannot save you from yourself.

Marriage does not inoculate you against heartbreak.

Marriage is not a guarantee of forever.

Marriage is not a guarantee of anything.

Are Shared Interests Important?

I learned everything I knew about true romance, relationships and love through watching movies, listening to songs and closely observing the world around me.

This is how I built a tower — no, an entire city of towers — filled to the brim with absurd notions and preposterous expectations.

One day, desperate to be happy, I demolished all that.

Just because something works for everyone else doesn't mean it works for me.

Just because something doesn't work for anyone doesn't mean it won't work for me.

Let me start from scratch. Let me raze the fantasy and the fairy tales and the stories and everyone else's voices.

What is it that I want?

My relationships and my needs are as unique and personal as my fingerprint.

For me, shared *values* are key, but shared *interests* are not incredibly important.

Different interests open my eyes to other things, reveal worlds I am unlikely to ever learn much about, present me with a new perspective and give us many, many brand new things to talk about at the end of a long day where he pursued what interests him and I pursued what interests me.

For other couples, shared interests and a day spent together, inseparable, is crucially important.

What I think is important and what others think is important does not matter. What matters is what works for you.

First Move

I am going to tell you something that will save you time, effort, heartbreak, struggle and frustration.

It will save you pain, stress and strife, tension and toil.

It might even save you from destruction.

Ready?

You cannot make anyone do anything.

If you want her to make the first move, you can say *"I wish you'd make the first move. That would be just dandy. It would be nifty. It would be splendid."*

One could argue that uttering this is in effect a move, but it's really very little effort.

After expressing it you can sit back, lounge, loiter, and be a spectator to what happens next.

This is all you can do.

Why Is Seeming Desperate Undesirable?

Despair is the opposite of confidence. It breeds carelessness, frenzy, haste. It is urgent, foolhardy, impetuous.

His back is to the wall.

If someone is desperate, his ability to discern is compromised. There is an absence of clear boundaries.

Without these things, neither he nor I know who he is.

I can't be in a relationship if I cannot see whom it is that I am loving.

Chancy

Many years ago a friend of mine was dating a poor guy and a rich guy.

She loved the poor guy but married the rich one because her parents insisted the choice would safeguard her future.

I have nothing against rich guys, but I do have something against this one. He beat her so badly so often that they greeted her by first name in the emergency room, where time and again she refused to press charges.

In the meantime, the poor guy worked on a passion project he sold to a large food company. The guy is intelligent and modest and lovely, but also now he is astoundingly rich.

You see, the future is chancy. It does not concern itself with our assumptions, our logic, our predictions, our certainty, the things that worry us or the plans that we make.

The present, instead, is right here, a bird in the hand. The present is more real, more secure and more clear than anything else on the planet.

If I have right now something special, my primal instinct is to make space for it.

I have faith — maybe too much — that things will work out. I don't need to know exactly how.

This is because most things don't turn out the way we think, and because most of what sorts itself out does so without my intervention.

More importantly, if I'm wrong and nothing works out, what I have left is the experience I had the courage to fully give myself to, instead of the regret of walking away from something beautiful.

Yes, yes. It's foolhardy of me to suggest you not concern yourself too much with the future, and instead seize the present.

You would not be the first person to consider me reckless.

It's just that to me, the worst kind of bargain I can think of striking is to willingly miss out on something both certain and special in exchange for something indistinct, vague and that might never take place.

How Do I Know It's Safe to Marry?

Get married. Don't get married. Either way I 100% guarantee you are not safe.

You will get hurt, feel lost, confused, betrayed, heartbroken. You will marry the wrong person.

You will marry the right person and the wrong one will turn out to be you.

Someone you love will disappoint you, in a big way or in a thousand minuscule secret ways. I can even tell you who.

Everyone. Everyone you love.

No one can live up to the trillion expectations we refuse to admit we have.

If you do nothing and retreat and remain circumscribed to your bedroom and stay under the covers you are still not safe. You will have instead relinquished everything that is beautiful.

You are not safe. You are not safe. Not ever. Now go live your life as if your death was certain. Because it is.

Online Dating

I find online dating really fun. I like meeting new people, and online dating gives you a reach that is difficult to accomplish any other way.

In other words, you meet people you wouldn't normally meet.

What I find difficult about it is that everyone is looking for something abstract, using sentences that have no subject.

Let me explain.

"I want to get married."

Or *"I want to have children."*

Or *"I am looking for a lover."*

Or they ask me *"What are you looking for?"*

To me, the question without a subject is almost impossible to answer.

If I meet a person and like him, I can say *"I want this person in my life".* Or *"I want this person to be my friend".*

Or, if there is a certain kind of chemistry, I might think *"This man. I really want him to be my lover".* Or even *"This guy. I want to marry him".*

But, wanting to get married without knowing to whom is difficult. I don't see myself ever getting married again but if the right person asks me, my answer might be *"I don't want to 'get married', but I want to marry you".*

This abstraction — this wanting of something without a subject — lends itself to a churn, to people cycling through people searching for someone who doesn't exist. It lends itself to having more expectations, to being easily disappointed, instead of being receptive.

It makes it very easy for the right person to be quickly discarded.

In the abstract, I can only vaguely articulate what I want and what I don't.

To be clearer and more certain I need to meet you and get to know you and then determine what it is that I want with you.

What If a Friend Declares She Loves You?

First I say thank you.

"Thank you so much for loving me."

Then I say, *"I love you too, so much. It's not the same kind of love, but you and your friendship are really important to me.*

"I anticipate that after this conversation things will get awkward between us.

"You matter to me so much that I am willing to let things get awkward, to work through this until things go back to normal. I hope you are too, because I don't want to lose you."

And then I say — *"And now, to kick things off, want to go catch a movie?".*

The Hunt

The worst advice I've ever heard that is most often repeated is "play hard to get".

Because, *"men like the hunt, and if you express your true feelings they will lose interest".*

Here is why this is terrible advice:

If you say "no" and the guy pushes you for "yes" you set your filter wrong: you attract men who feel it's necessary to override what you say.

Do you see? You attract guys who feel they have a right over you and who are comfortable ignoring your boundaries.

Then you wonder why all your relationships are so garbled and fraught with drama.

Instead, communicate as clearly as you can. *"I like you." "I find you attractive."*

Will some guys lose interest if you do this?

Sure.

This is excellent, because those are not the guys you want.

You want the ones who find clear communication totally hot.

Who are excited you like them too.

Who find it attractive to be in a relationship where no one is playing games.

The reward is the company of a man who digs who you are and listens for what you want, instead of one who just wants you to be a stand-in for whatever it is he needs, and a thing that belongs to him.

Setting the Tone

The beginning of a relationship sets the tone for its very nature, structure and composition.

This is when I ask myself what kind of relationship I want.

This is when I can be who I am or pretend to be things I'm not.

How plausible will it be for me to be this person that I'm not weeks, months, years from now?

You need time alone, Dushka. Establish this now.

This is when I can express what I like, or pretend to like what he likes. If I pretend to like what he likes, that might be difficult for me to sustain long term.

Actually, I don't really like watching sports on TV. I told you that I did to seem cool, but I'd rather be doing anything else.

This is when I can flatter. I can be honest or I can be less so, in which case I am giving the indication that I like things I actually don't.

I know I told you I liked you clean-shaven but actually I love when you're scruffy and scratchy.

It's better to be honest: it represents me more clearly, it is easier to keep track of what I say, it's viable to sustain.

Most of all this way I know you want to be with me rather than with the nonexistent person I am pretending to be.

Should I Be Afraid of Love?

Love is brutal.

It makes you vulnerable. It leaves you exposed.

It removes any protective shield you might have managed to develop, leaving your vital organs at the mercy of someone vicious, bloodthirsty and fully armed.

Love leaves you wide open — on the line.

You should most definitely be afraid of love.

Love anyway.

Should I Avoid Commitment?

Everyone is different.

For some people, commitment feels like a prison.

For others, it feels like they are finally free.

Some people cannot imagine life with only one partner.

Others want one person to love. Multiple partners feels like too much to manage.

There is no should. There is no everyone. What do you want? What works for you?

Find that. Do that.

Things to Remember During a Relationship

Possessive

Let's say that a guy cheats on me. This hurts me so much it changes me. I begin to doubt my worth, become suspicious and determine that to ensure this never happens to me again I need to control the man I am with.

I go through his phone and through his things. I tell him he cannot have women friends and that I always want to know where he is.

This accomplishes the opposite of what I want. At first he is understanding, even somewhat accommodating. But quickly he feels trapped, suffocated.

Despite truly loving me this inevitably results in him wanting to get away from me. I wouldn't blame him.

The above is an example of me placing the burden of my insecurities squarely on the other person, expecting another to change his behavior so I can hurt less.

This is the equivalent of feeling my nose itch and scratching my shoulder. It's just not where the fix is.

There is only one way to deal with relationship insecurity and that is to be possessive of it. This insecurity is mine and only mine. As such, only I can work to understand it, manage it, talk to it, soothe it, and ultimately extinguish it.

Compromise/Sacrifice

Compromise: You want something and I want another and we find a middle ground.

Positive outcome: we are both happy.

Risk: this middle ground doesn't really satisfy either one of us.

Sacrifice: You want something and I want another and I give up on what I want so you can have what you want.

Positive outcome: my sacrifice is a part of a larger system in this relationship and I know that as I give to you, you give to me — not as a transaction but as a team.

Risk: this sacrifice is badly calibrated and plants in the relationship a debt that cannot be repaid.

Are My Feelings Real or an Illusion?

Ah, that's easy.

Always, without exception, an illusion.

For at least the first few months of any relationship, maybe longer, people are a stand-in for who we want them to be.

What you "love" doesn't come from them — it comes from inside of you.

You don't really know the person, which means that what you think you are seeing is not real.

What you are feeling is an optical illusion conceived by yearning; a fantasy.

You have all these ideas of what another should be and find a mirror for what you think you want reflected back at you.

You are falling in love with a character of your own fabrication, after which you proceed — quickly or over the years — to disappoint yourself.

This is why it's so risky to say "I love you" too early. Because the person that you fervently declare your love to wants to make sure you are in love with who they really are and not something you have inadvertently fabricated.

This is also why it's so common to quickly fall insanely in love only to come to your senses as you discover the other person has the audacity to be who they actually are.

Is Cheating Sometimes Necessary?

I am not and will not ever be in a position where I can take a moral high ground.

I am not interested in judging anyone.

If you are going to cheat, cheat. If you are going to lie, lie. When you do, keep your eyes wide open.

Healing from anything you do to yourself at the bare minimum requires that you own up to your decisions, that you be fully accountable for what you have done.

If you tell yourself "it was necessary" then on top of lying to someone who loves you you are lying to yourself.

That is really hard to come back from.

Yeah, I Do Want a Label

I once wanted to be free and decided I didn't want labels. I was cool that way, chill. Open. Whatever.

Except, I did. I did want a label. I had no idea what to expect and the situation I had placed myself in the middle of was bringing out the worst in me: I was anxious, stressed, clinging.

I was shackled by what I was calling freedom.

I decided that the best thing I could do for myself was name what I wanted — articulate it — and then ask for it. That anything less than that was me not fairly representing my own interests.

Asking for what you want as clearly as possible leads to losing all those who don't want the same thing, and this is so scary but delivers, with laser like infallibility, everything you're looking for.

Was it too much to ask for me to tell the man currently known as Boyfriend that I am monogamous and as such require exclusivity?

Do you know who has the answer to that? Who is the worldwide authority of what is and what isn't too much for me to ask for?

Me.

Or, in this case, you.

What's the Dirtiest Thing You've Ever Done?

A couple of weeks ago I was talking to a friend at work who confessed that eating popcorn in bed was her "guilty pleasure".

My response was that I never, not ever, associate "guilt" with "pleasure". That to me sounds like self-sabotage. There are many delicious things to experience, and feeling guilty about them would undercut my ability to enjoy them.

What an absurd way to live.

I feel similarly about the notion of doing something "dirty". Sex isn't dirty. Sex is awesome, and primal, and it makes me feel connected to something fundamental. At its best it reminds me of a cardinal thing within me, an axis. *Dushka, this is who you are. This is what you want.*

I had sex with a guy once. I bring him up specifically because I did things with him I had not done before and have not done since. It doesn't matter if they were wild or kinky or exotic. It doesn't matter what they were.

What matters is that sex with him made me feel electric, alive. It made me feel like I wanted to do everything, like I could bestow pleasure upon someone, like I had the power to make someone who mattered to me gasp with delight and surprise.

He in turn made me feel what I can only refer to as bliss.

The time I spent with him felt like a respite from all the things that weigh on me. Like we could take a vacation from our life to give something of ourselves to each other. It felt like what happens to you when you overcome your insecurities and your fear.

He felt like a reward.

It's not just that it wasn't dirty. It's that, at least to me, it was sacred.

What I want to tell you is that considering sex dirty severs you from something in you that is elemental, intrinsic to who you are. Don't do that to yourself.

If there ever was a sin, it's to turn our back on the pleasure and beauty that we were designed to give and to receive.

The Price of White Lies

If you tell me you're busy rather than *"I really don't like parties"* then you are not really letting me get to know you or understand you.

If I ask you how you're doing and you say *"I'm fine"* and you are not, you are shutting me out.

If you tell me you love something you don't love, you make it hard for me to learn how to get you the right gift.

If you tell me this dress looks great on me when it doesn't, you are doing me a disservice.

White lies create distance between us. They might spare me in that moment, but in the long run no white lie is kind.

Can You Love More Than One Person?

When my brother had his first baby girl, my niece, and I held her in my arms I felt a love I had never felt before, so fierce it hurt my chest. I cried standing there nuzzling her.

When he called a few years later to tell me they were having another baby I fretted I would not feel the same way. How could I replicate a love so gigantic? But then I met my nephew and realized I had nothing to worry about. I held this new baby and felt my heart expand.

It takes a few seconds for me to think of at least two exes I still love.

It takes about that same amount of time to recognize that this love does not threaten my love for Boyfriend at all, since everyone resides in a different untouchable space.

It's not that every love has its place in my heart; it's that it feels like every love has all of it.

This abundance, this heart multiplicity, has nothing to do with being polyamorous. I am monogamous and even from here I can clearly see that we are each given an infinite capacity for a love that cannot affect the other.

We can love many people and have each love be its own sovereign universe.

It's such a privilege, to possess expanding hearts, and pretending it is not so for an illusion of safety would negate the very best in us.

Can a Toxic Relationship Be a Comfort Zone?

Bingo.

Most definitely.

We associate "comfort" with happiness but it's closer to "familiar".

"Familiar" is not always good.

Comfort is related to convenience, to alleviation, to complacency, to a sense of security that comes from what we know.

What we know is not necessarily healthy.

This is why toxic relationships are hard to fix and so hard to get away from.

You know what they say — better the devil that you know, than the devil that you don't.

It takes courage to venture towards the devil that you don't.

It's the only way out.

Bored

You say you are bored with your relationship, but afraid no one else will ever want you if you leave.

Boredom comes from repeatedly allowing fear to be the driver of the decisions that I make.

If I am worried or afraid and this becomes the reason I keep myself from doing something, my life becomes increasingly circumscribed.

Boredom does not come from other people.

If I feel anyone out there is boring me, what is actually happening is that I'm bored with myself.

The reason this is important to identify is because if something is coming from inside of me I will take it everywhere I go — I will go through a lot of time and effort to cycle important people out of my life, only to find I eventually get bored with the new people too.

If I was bored with my relationship the first thing I would do is ask myself if I consider this person I have been with to be worth preserving.

Nothing is less boring than attempting to revitalize a relationship or successfully transitioning out of it while remaining friends with a person who has been an important part of my life for so long.

The other option is to recognize that me being worried I will never find another person is precisely what is perpetuating a boring life.

The antidote to boredom is to look at all the things that scare and worry me and do them anyway.

Boundary or Control?

Imagine I'm dating a man who likes going out at night. I like him and going out with him is fun. He shows me many things I'm not normally exposed to — we go to new restaurants, dancing, the theater, stay up late.

As the novelty wears off, I begin to notice this is having an impact on my life. I can't get up early to write, I'm tired when I get to work, instead of going to yoga regularly I skip it to catch up on sleep.

This is taking a toll on my health.

One day I tell him that while I like him I need to adjust the dynamic he has become used to. I can go out sometimes, but not as frequently and not as late.

This is a new boundary. It's not consistent with the behavior I've shown him and yet it is just right. Boundaries are not static, and they belong to me. They are about my limits, what I'm willing or not willing to do, and as such it doesn't matter what other people think of them.

His reaction will determine our compatibility.

If he respects my boundary he might say *"Yeah. Your health comes first and this adjustment sounds reasonable".* He might add *"I have been feeling overextended myself".*

If he does not respect my boundary, he might say *"I don't like this"* or even *"this has an impact over the relationship I imagined".*

I need to remain firm in my boundary. This is unrelated to how much I like him. If I say *"OK, let's just keep going out"* I am putting my health at risk. Given enough time, I will become someone different from the person he met.

If you don't respect your own boundaries, you compromise who you are. For a short period of time you might keep the other person, at the cost of losing yourself.

Now, imagine if instead of saying *"I need to adjust this dynamic"* I say *"I need you to change. You cannot go out every night — it's not good for either of us."*

Instead of focusing the action on me, I want to adjust his way of life to suit my needs. Or, if you prefer, I want to adjust his way of life "for his own good".

Either way, that's not a boundary. That's attempting to exercise control on another person, and it is neither respectful nor healthy.

Is It Possible to Overcome Jealousy?

For me, jealousy — my poison, my temporary insanity, my ruination — was a sign of insecurity but it was also a tangle, a labyrinth, a morass.

I felt that if I was not jealous I was not being responsible, not playing the vigilant role I was taught and expected to play. I was not "taking care of my man".

A lack of jealousy was a guarantee he'd cheat on me. I was asking for it. It was what I deserved for the sin that was my blind trust and absence of suspicion.

The possibility of being cheated on implied not just a breach of trust, but an insult to my intelligence. Somehow the wool had been pulled over my eyes, which would confirm me as a fool.

Finally, being cheated on was uncontested proof that someone else was better than me. More beautiful, more lovable, sexier, more adequate.

I would not only have to deal with the pain of betrayal, but also contend with the evidence of my inferiority.

The truth is that other people will do what they will do and I cannot stop them, even if I lived (and I did) in a constant state of high alert and rampant paranoia.

The truth is cheating is on the other person and not on me, and my only work — my only work — is to trust that I am worth loving.

The truth is that being cheated on and my worth are not related. Incredible, amazing people get cheated on, which reveals more about the cheater than about them.

This is how I untangled that mess, how I escaped my labyrinth. I seldom feel jealousy now and when I do I thank it for trying to protect me.

"I'm OK," I tell it. *"Thank you, you beautiful monster, for struggling to keep me safe. You and I are going to be just fine."*

Not True for Everyone

When I am in love with one person it's practically impossible for me to fathom having sex with another.

I very easily like — and love — others, and find other men attractive, even desirable, but I really don't feel like shagging anyone else. Whenever I have, it's been the clearest sign of all that my relationship is over.

This trait made it hard for me to grasp a concept that is really quite simple: not everyone is like me.

Many people love deeply *and* find sex with others to be quite appetizing.

Let me put it in more obvious terms: just because someone wants to have sex with other people does not necessarily imply they don't truly love you.

Why is this worth noting? Because understanding that you can love me deeply and want to have sex with others hurts less than feeling that you wanting to have sex with others means you don't love me enough.

(To be fair, he could say he was deeply dismayed that you don't love him enough to just deal with the fact he wants to sleep with others. And you know you do. You do, but this slams right into who you are.)

I love this recurring epiphany that just because something is true for me doesn't mean it's true for everyone — but I extra love it when it means it hurts a bit less.

So now my next step is to remember that I don't have the ability to either change or control another. I can rant, I can rave, I can live a life of perpetual friction, pain and unhappiness, but I cannot change the other person. I have to start with me.

As such, *Dushka, is loving someone who loves you and will always want to have sex with other women something you can accept, embrace, live with?*

Only one person on the planet can answer this question: me.

Or, if this is your plight, you.

Expectations

Let's say you put a great deal of effort in celebrating your partner's birthday and he does nothing for yours.

This hurts. Do you get angry?

This is an expectation.

You expect another person will do something specific.

The first thing I do when I have one of these (which is all the time) is remind myself my expectations are on me and not on anyone else.

What this means is that he is not to blame. He is not disappointing me. I am doing this to myself.

The reason why this matters is because this is how I suffer less: I cannot change him but can assume responsibility for myself.

The second thing I would do is put into practice clear communication. I would tell him, *"Birthdays are really important to me and it would mean a lot to me if you celebrated mine. I'd love a gift and dinner and your presence and attention".*

I would not present this as a demand, I would not be angry and I would not suggest a quid pro quo (I do it for you and therefore you should do it for me) but as an independent, stand-alone request.

This is because if I make a big deal of his birthday that is not on him, but on me. I can't use something I'm solely responsible for, something he didn't ask for, as leverage.

After making my wishes clear, I would embrace that no man — no human — will love me the way I want him to love me. He will love me the way he loves.

What this means is he might feel like he does not want to celebrate my birthday despite knowing it matters to me.

Here, I have one choice left to make: is this a big deal? Can I live with this, or will it hurt me every time?

If I realize that in the context of everything else he does, celebrating my birthday really doesn't matter, then I will let this one slide — forever, every year — for my own peace of mind.

Maybe my birthday can become the official day I celebrate with all my friends, without him.

If instead I realize that I just can't, that this happens to be central to my happiness and the health of our relationship, then I would conclude we are not compatible.

This is when I would set him free to find a beautiful woman who will never even remember his birthday or their anniversaries and find myself a gem of a man who will insist on painting the world red to commemorate the day I was born.

Jealousy Does Not Equal Love

If he doesn't love you but gets jealous it means he doesn't love you and is a jealous guy.

Jealousy does not = love.

Jealousy = noxious.

I understand this is difficult to put together. I believed many things about life and love that I later discovered were not true.

Way beyond not being true, believing them was poisoning my life.

Examples:

If I feel it, that means it's real.

If I am never vulnerable, I will always be safe.

I have a soul mate and when I find him everything will fall into place.

I must play hard to get.

Guys who like sex are virile. Women who like sex are sluts.

Happy people are happy all the time.

If you don't feel jealous, you don't love me.

If you do feel jealous, that means you love me.

A little jealousy is healthy.

If you are not possessive, you don't love me.

If you loved me, you'd want to own me.

If you don't want to control me, you don't love me.

Fear = respect.

Always.

Never.

If I feel insecure, it's your job to make me feel better by adapting your behavior to my requirements.

If you cheat on me, you don't love me.

If you want to sleep with other people, you don't love me.

If I wear a short skirt I'm being provocative and therefore "asking for it."

If I want to go out with my friends, they are more important to me than you.

I should be your priority.

It's your job to make me happy.

You will save me.

Love conquers all.

Love is all we need.

I want your love to be unconditional.

My love for you is unconditional, and that's a good thing.

We never fight, and that's a good thing.

Never go to bed angry.

Relationships take a ton of work.

Fully understanding how each of these statements is a lie changed my life.

I offer them here in the hope they do the same for you.

Are Relationships About Compromise?

You are compatible with someone when you are able to easily, effortlessly coexist in harmony.

Or, in the absence of harmony, you are willing to evaluate your preferences and expectations to arrive at a place where harmony can be established.

You are not compatible when coexisting in harmony is not possible and the effort to get there, rather than making you better, begins to feel like you are always compromising who you are.

Compromise is, by definition, "meeting you halfway". You want something and I want another and we find a middle ground. In an ideal world we are both happy. It's just that it seldom works out that way.

More often what we arrive at satisfies neither one of us.

It's for this reason that I don't believe relationships are about compromise. It's not that I would be unwilling to. It's that it's a fallacy. In the short term you feel like a responsible, mature adult but in the long term this type of accommodation breeds dissatisfaction, a sense of having sacrificed too much, and resentment.

All these things lodge in undisclosed nooks and erupt in inconvenient moments, like an active volcano in the middle of a bustling city.

Relationships to me are instead about the ability to learn more about yourself by seeing you through the eyes of another. Then I do what I do because it will make me a better person. My effort is not a giving in, but something I do to better myself.

That, and accepting the person you are with for exactly who he is.

End of My Rope

I had a friend who used to drop in unannounced. The first time it happened I felt mildly imposed upon but pleased to see her. After that I felt like diving under the bed but pretended I was happy about her unplanned arrivals.

I want to be a good person. I want to be generous. I want to do right by my friends. I want them to feel supported by me.

It's maybe for these reasons that I waited until I felt desperate to establish boundaries. By that point I was angry, resentful, feeling like I was being taken advantage of.

If you wait until you're at the end of your rope to handle something like this, you come at it when any reservoir of patience or grace has run out.

Maybe the solution was to establish these boundaries before things got to this point.

Boundaries are not, *"Hey, you have gone too far".* Ideally they mean, *"This is the line. Please remain on the other side so that you going too far does not happen".*

This is why I announce early on that I am an introvert, a writer who needs time to write, and just in general quirky as hell.

I need lots of space and I love you, but please, don't come over without letting me know.

Why Do You Love Me?

When someone asks *"Why do you love me?"* what they are asking for is your attention. A verbal snuggle. A word caress.

This is an appeal, a petition.

So step back and take a good look. Extend. Offer. Give. Deliver.

Deliver on this plea from the person that you love.

Because oh my god the spiral of your earlobe.

Because look — look at the lines on the palm of your hand. I want to trace them until I feel your life line line up with mine.

Here. Let's put our hands flat against each other.

Because, look at the curve of your neck — your leg — your waist — the arch of your foot. How could I not love someone who carries curves like you carry curves?

Because, I can barely breathe when you look at me like that.

Because you want. Because you try. Because you search. Because you are hungry like me, afraid like me, contradictory like me. Because you are nothing like me.

Because I like me when I'm with you.

But mostly because I don't need a reason. Because. Just because.

Because is all I will ever need to love you.

What If We Don't Want to Live Together?

Your relationship belongs to you. You can design this relationship any way you want.

What is right for the two of you? What works?

The answer to this might be unconventional or atypical. It might feel "not normal".

The fact that what works for you is not what works for "everyone" does not matter.

What matters is that your relationship needs you to give it the best chance at thriving, and for many, many people, living apart works much better than living together.

Can I Ask My Boyfriend to Stop Drinking?

I met the man I currently refer to as Boyfriend online. On his dating profile he clearly stated he was a smoker.

I reached out to him because his writing made me laugh and I thought a date with him would be fun.

The fact that he smoked did not factor into my decision because I had not considered a date with him could turn into a relationship.

As we got to know each other I noticed the impact smoking had on him. I didn't like it.

I thought for a long time if I needed to say anything or not. I went into the relationship knowing he smoked. How could I now protest if he had always been forthcoming?

I decided saying nothing would be unhealthy. Honest communication is important and he needed to know how I felt.

"I think the fact that you smoke is affecting your health," I said. *"The more time goes by the more likely it is that it will have a serious impact on you and my plan is to stick around long enough to witness that. It bothers me that you are doing something that is bad for you."*

I did not ask him to stop. In fact, I very clearly stated I expected nothing and that I just wanted him to know.

I made him uncomfortable.

After this declaration of mine he continued to smoke and while I was a bit disappointed my words had not had any effect on him I let the matter go.

About five months later he said he wanted to stop smoking. He added that it was becoming increasingly complicated logistically, and that he was getting into Crossfit and it was affecting his workouts.

I told him I loved him no matter what and he assured me his decision was unrelated to me.

It took several attempts for him to kick the habit. Through them all I said nothing, judged nothing, gave him no attitude if after several weeks of triumphantly managing not to smoke he'd excuse himself to go outside. As much as I wanted to help or encourage I minded my own business and let him fight his battle without my nosy intervention.

We cannot demand that others change to accommodate what we want, even if we believe that what we want is in their interest. We can only change ourselves.

This is the paradox of love: you can't control another person's behavior and yet love will transform you.

The trick is to take people exactly as they are and communicate who we are as clearly and honestly as possible so they can do the same for us.

Fundamental

I am going to tell you something really important: something fundamental. So much so that the day I understood it, it changed the way I perceive the world.

Ready?

Love is not supposed to hurt.

If it hurts, something somewhere is off and needs to be reconsidered.

Thrashing

When I am with someone who thinks I am not good enough and I am trying, trying to be, it feels like I'm thrashing in freezing, choppy water, thrashing and drowning. *I can't do this. I can't do this anymore.*

When I am with someone who thinks I am enough and encourages me to be better — acceptance and encouragement can and do happily coexist — it feels like I am floating on my back in the middle of a vast, warm, peaceful ocean.

I don't bother asking myself why this guy thinks I am not good enough or *what on earth is wrong with me* or *what the heck is happening.*

I get away from the thrashing, anxious feeling and move towards the warm, supported feeling.

It's not just that striving to be accepted for who I am is not interesting.

It's that I simply don't have the stamina.

Nothing to Do With Her

I have a friend who gets angry when her boyfriend goes out with his friends. It's not that she tells him he can't. It's that she suffers when he does.

She believes that him going out without her is evidence that he would rather be with his friends than with her.

"Do you believe it's possible," I say, *"That him wanting to go out with them means he wants to go out with them, unrelated to you?"*

I know her boyfriend. He is completely in love with her. And, sometimes he wants to go out without her. The fact that this hurts her so much makes him feel powerless, frustrated, and ultimately, suffocated.

He believes, and I agree, that he cannot respond to this by not going out. This is something she needs to sort out herself.

She cannot reconcile that him going out without her has nothing to do with her. She cannot believe he would go out despite knowing it hurts her.

Her insecurity is warping her perception.

She cannot recognize reality and is in a world of pain, not over something that is happening, but over something she believes.

The Same Mistake

Maybe I'm daft or distracted or stubborn or can't see things as quickly as I should but I make the same mistake over and over a thousand times before learning anything at all.

Maybe it's that my mistakes feel so delicious.

Take relationships. I used to fall for someone and immediately say *"Here, this is my life. You can just take it".*

This is love, right? Total, unconditional, selfless love.

It took years — YEARS — before something inside me clicked and *wait a minute Dushka why on earth are you so willing — no, eager — to give yourself over to someone and call it "love"?* This is codependency and it's unhealthy and it is painful as hell and no one is better equipped at taking care of you and looking out for you and loving you than you.

Please, please we have to stop doing that.

Even after this awareness, even after this plea of me from me, even then…well.

How tempting, to call this pattern my destiny. To repeat the same mistake over and over and keep learning so very much from the exact same lesson, until one day I see it coming a mile away.

Hello, old friend. Here we are again.

We've come so far, Dushka. So, tell me. What's it going to be this time?

Not Always Happy

The key to a happy marriage is accepting that you will not make me happy, that I will not make you happy, that we are not perfect, and that nothing here is ideal.

The key to a happy marriage is accepting you as fallible, accepting me as fallible, accepting life as fallible.

The key to a happy marriage — and perhaps to a happy life — is to be secure and comfortable in the knowledge that we will not always be happy.

Abandoned

I have a friend who is convinced everyone will sooner or later leave him. He will end up stranded, abandoned, alone.

This belief taints his relationships. He is aloof, dismissive, cold, to avoid getting too close.

Or, he is possessive, holds on too tightly, tries to control, becomes abusive as he becomes increasingly afraid of the power of his own prophecy.

Either way, it becomes painful and self destructive to anyone who has the audacity to try to stay.

This is how we create, conjure, bring to life all the things we fear the most.

We are the only ones responsible for the traps we set for ourselves and as such the only ones with the ability to find the way out.

Why Won't He Commit?

I am averse to commitment.

Let me give you some perspective from the brain of a person who does not want to commit.

It doesn't matter.

It doesn't matter why a guy won't commit. You can spend your whole life wondering, suffering and making excuses for this lack of interest in committing.

What matters instead are the questions you can actually answer, because they are in you and not in him.

Is what you want commitment? If so, why are you still with a man who is withholding precisely what you want?

You are not stuck. You are not tethered. This is not your destiny.

Is his love minus this commitment that you want enough? If so, stop once and for all with this concern over his inability to commit and love him. Just love him. And let him love you his way, not yours.

Is this commitment you want so badly from him something you cannot live without? Is this your deal breaker, despite his love?

Then, please. Save yourself pain. Save yourself time. Stop making a man who loves you feel like his love is perpetually inadequate. Stop asking questions you can never answer and walk away.

Love is joyful. It's a pleasure. The world is full of people who want exactly what you want, whatever that is.

It's just that they can't find you if you are inexplicably beholden to the one person who will never be who you want him to be.

You or Me?

You and I get into a fight.

We fight because I was expecting you to do something, and you did not.

This expectation — was it an agreement, or just something I assumed was going to happen?

What do I need to work on?

Our communication, or on me?

You do something that makes me madly jealous.

Where does this insane jealousy come from?

Is this your behavior or my insecurity?

Who do I need to work on, us or me?

Learn to make this elusive distinction. Where is the source of the problem?

Am I certain it's not me?

Best Girlfriend Ever

When Boyfriend has to work late it's because he's responsible, not because he derives pleasure from being at the office instead of with me.

If he looks at his phone and I can't see the screen it's because he's private, not because there's anything on that device that he doesn't want me to see.

Or, if he doesn't want me to see it, it does not concern me.

Boyfriend finds other women attractive and sometimes develops crushes on people other than me, which far from affecting me is proof of a delightful vitality.

Boyfriend goes to parties without me because he likes parties more than I do and goes out with his friends because it's fun. It makes me happy that he's happy. I never feel he's choosing something over me.

When we fight I don't think he wants to hurt me. I think he wants me to understand something.

I trust him, assume he operates with the best of intentions and don't take things personally, which means I set myself free from anger, resentment, suspicion and drama.

I don't know if my aversion to drama makes me the best girlfriend ever but it sure makes life easier for me.

Aggressive Rejection

When I try to change or control another person — to make them more like what I want them to be — what I am really saying is *"to me, you are not enough"*.

"I do not accept who you already are."

"Making" someone do something cannot be done, but also it's an aggressive rejection of the person he already is.

Social Media or Me

Do you believe that if someone is super jealous and wants you all to himself he must be completely in love with you?

Do you think that someone who checks in on you and calls to ask where you are every couple of hours is crazy about you?

Do you believe that if your partner says *"delete all your social media or I will leave you"* and you say no, this sounds like you are "choosing" social media over him?

If this is what you believe, you are confusing love with control.

You are missing an enormous red sign that says "abuser".

Anyone who puts you in a place where you have to choose by threatening to leave is someone to get away from.

Fixer Uppers

If he says he loves me with all his heart and I don't love myself I will have a hard time believing he is telling me the truth.

If he has no interest in anyone else but every move I make is suspicious and vigilant I will strangle his feelings for me.

If I think I can change or improve him (for his own good, of course) and nag, the nagging will take away the air he needs to breathe. I am in essence telling him that who he already is is not good enough.

People are not fixer uppers.

If there are things he wants to do and I don't "let him", even if I know they are bad for him, I am threatening his sovereignty.

Love does not conquer all. It is almost meek when it comes up against the powerhouse of our insecurities.

Is Marriage Important?

I was married for over 15 years, after which I got a divorce.

I realize I assumed marriage would protect me. It would extinguish my internal insatiable pursuit for who knows what and for the rest of my life shield me from heartbreak.

Marriage was supposed to be absolution and the answer to so many questions and instead it taught me that the only person who can protect me from myself is me, that my insatiable pursuits are mine to manage (with as much grace as I can muster) and that heartbreak is both inevitable and necessary.

I am in a relationship now and we have love, commitment, camaraderie and a shared belief that we are worth sticking it out. I believe marriage has nothing to contribute to my relationship that it doesn't already have and, as such, I do not at all consider it important.

Fighting Dirty

Fighting can be dirty. It can be full of low blows. It can aim to hurt. It can aim to win. It can intend to diminish the other person, making her feel less important, like she is always wrong, like she doesn't matter.

It means weaponizing something originally offered to you with love.

It means shutting out, subduing, defeating, destroying.

It means treating the person you love like an adversary.

Fighting well is healthy. It means establishing your boundaries. It means standing up for yourself. It means explaining your position clearly and respectfully, and trying your best to put yourself in the other person's shoes. It means compassion. It means understanding.

Fighting well is necessary for every relationship, and it's a relationship builder.

Why Is Gaslighting So Disturbing?

When someone tries to manipulate you, they attempt to manage or influence you.

Manipulation is a form of control, something like *"please, believe only me"*.

If you loosen the hold a manipulator has on you, you find you have yourself as a reference against what to believe.

Gaslighting is a process by which a person makes another doubt their sanity. Something like *"please, do not believe yourself"*.

If you loosen the hold a gaslighter has on you, you doubt your own handle on reality.

A gaslighter has an impact on your ability to trust yourself.

Brutal Truth

What you say is completely different from what I hear.

What he says: *Hey! I can't see you tonight! I'm going to hang out with my friends.*

What she hears: *I would rather be with my friends than be with you.*

What she says: *I am so tired. I need space. I am going to spend Sunday alone, but maybe we can do something in the evening.*

What he hears: *I don't want to be with you.*

What she says: *I am working late again tonight.*

What he hears: *My work is more important to me than you.*

How do you suppose things get garbled so badly?

How is what one person hears so different from what another person says?

You know how? By making things that have nothing to do with me about me.

Nothing confuses things more, makes me suffer more or destroys more relationships than believing that whatever it is you need is directly related to me.

And that, my friend, is the brutal truth about relationships.

Get Away

Get away from anyone who is cruel to you, who wants to diminish you, who puts you down, who tries to control you, who hurts you or who frightens you.

It doesn't matter who they are.

Priorities

If I meet a man and he has kids I sure hope his kids come first. I used to be that kid, and my father made sure his first consideration was me. His wife didn't need him like I needed him. Men who put their kids first are the kind of men I want.

If I meet a man and he has a passion, a deep interest that drives him, that makes him feel alive and filled with purpose, I sure hope his passion comes first. This means we will always have something new to talk about, that he will always have some interesting insight, but it also means we will love each other and support each other without being codependent.

I need to be important to the people I am with but I am very comfortable not being their priority.

I don't think there is any other notion quite as healthy or quite as liberating as the fact that I am not the center of the world.

What Makes a Relationship "Toxic"?

I love you so much. I am going to isolate you from everyone who loves you so the only person you have is me.

I love you so much. I am going to keep you small so that I never risk losing you.

I love you so I will undermine you so that you stay with me.

I love you but I don't trust you.

I love you and for some reason I can no longer trust myself.

I love you and I am afraid of you.

I love you and I can't talk to you.

I love you and I can't tell you the truth.

I love you and you know exactly how to hurt me.

I love you so I am going to constantly criticize you — you know. So I can make you better.

I love you and feel you love me only when we are locked in a battle. We have to be fighting for me to feel you still care.

I love you so I will forget what is important to me so we can do only what is important to you.

You would if you loved me.

I love you and you exhaust me.

I love you and I'm angry because you are not making me happy.

I love you and I want everything to forever stay the same.

Reflection

A person's attitude towards me tells me more about their attitude towards themselves than about what I am worth as a person.

A person's behavior is more a reflection of who they are than of my value.

The better I understand this, the lighter I become.

What to Do If He's Going Away

Resolve to become a better version of yourself. The better you are the better your relationship.

Learn something new every day.

Analyze the areas where you might be dependent and work on becoming independent. Unburden your relationship.

Identify, develop and explore your own interests. This will add to your life and to your relationship a new dimension, more textured, more faceted.

Get really fit. It's for your brain but your body will thank you.

If you get busy doing these things the time he spends away will be over before you know it.

Should We Share a Bank Account?

One of my favorite Burning Man principles is "Radical Self-Reliance." If you plan to survive in an extreme environment you have to make sure you are fully responsible for yourself.

Everyone looks out for one another, and you rely on you.

Every burner I know packs extra supplies for others: water, food, even extra costumes or a coat. But you leave for Black Rock Desert certain that the person who's got your back is you.

You should be prepared to make it on your own.

From what I have seen in marriages, when there is one bank account there is one person taking care of finances. The other becomes financially disengaged.

Where is your money? How is it being spent? Are you saving? Investing?

Or are you putting all the burden of financial decisions on someone else?

A good relationship is based on total trust — that is a given.

What I am against is an arrangement that fosters codependency, compromising self-reliance.

Sharing Secrets

I don't think it would be accurate to say I share my secrets with my partner because I don't keep anything to myself.

What I share with Boyfriend is a stream of consciousness, my unfiltered inside voice, a wide open window into even the thoughts and impulses I don't ever intend to act upon.

I can't think of a single thing I'd ever feel unable to tell him.

I in fact can't think of having a relationship with a significant other where I would be hesitant to share anything about me.

What would be the point of a relationship like that?

Why Is My Boyfriend Heartless?

I used to spend a whole lot of time and energy attempting to decode why people around me did the things they did. I realized one day this was a losing battle.

We are not equipped to know what goes on in other people's brains.

I could, however, attempt to decode why I did what I did. I'm not saying this was easy, but at least it was possible, and possible felt like an improvement over being frustrated and perplexed with questions I would never find answers to.

I lacked the power to know *"why does he…?"* but I did possess the ability to explore *"why do I…?".*

So I worked at turning every single question I had about other people back onto me.

I would forever be unable to tell why my boyfriend seemed to have an on/off switch for his love.

So the question became *"Why do I feel that someone heartless is good enough for me?".*

My life has improved dramatically since that day I decided any question I ever asked about another was really about me.

Why Stay If You're Not Compatible?

Because everyone has told you love conquers all. Right? Right?

And, if love doesn't conquer all, where does that leave me?

Because if you could only change this or that about yourself or about the other person, everything would be so perfect.

Because you want to be open to change.

Because you tell yourself you love this person and are willing to put in the work.

Because this is so difficult and such a struggle — all I want is for this to work — and maybe someday it will.

Maybe if I try just a little bit harder. Maybe if I try just a little bit longer.

It's just around the corner, I think.

Even though it's been years.

Because it's been years and I have already invested so much.

Because love is love — it's so important — so maybe I can relinquish or compromise and somehow get there from here.

Because, isn't everything negotiable? We can work this out, right?

Right?

Because won't change — my own evolution — make me a better person? Aren't we supposed to be receptive, elastic, willing?

Because I already know this is not going to work, but I want to know — to know for certain — that I tried everything.

Fallible

If I have a hard line against being lied to and am lied to and in response I act categorical, absolute, implacable, unyielding, then it's possible that what broke as a result of this breach of trust can never be repaired.

If I am clear that I don't like being deceived but recognize human beings are all fallible, that I too have been known to lie, maybe I can identify that my relationship needs work and that we are a system we can repair together.

It's possible to come out on the other side with a stronger, more authentic dynamic than the one we once had.

Of course, it depends a lot on the people, and the situation, and what happened that caused the fracture in trust. But assuming that the person before me will never fail to act impeccably is, in my experience, not taking into account our fallibility, our natural inclination towards making ourselves seem better than we really are.

Is It Wrong to Lie to Make Someone Happy?

Do you mean you want to adapt, alter or change reality to suit your purpose, whatever that purpose may be?

Do you mean managing or influencing something without another person's knowledge?

Do you mean the other person cannot handle reality and that their happiness requires your expert intervention?

This is a condescending maneuver, an act of control, and it's the definition of manipulation.

Lonely

You are dating someone you don't love because you are lonely.

Do you know what? I can't judge you. I can't judge anyone — on what authority, if I myself have made every mistake in the book?

Feeling lonely is horrible. It feels like drowning — the only thing I want is to keep my head above water. I want to survive.

Sometimes to do so I hold on to the wrong person.

I believe this is something we have all done.

Do you know what I learned in doing so? That loneliness is an inside job. Trying to heal it with an outside fix doesn't work.

Loneliness feels like it can be addressed with the company of other people, but it can't. This is why you can feel lonely in a room full of others. This is why you can feel lonely even if you have many friends.

Loneliness is a fracture you have to mend inside of you.

Nothing makes me feel more alone than being in an unfulfilling relationship.

Nothing makes me feel more alone than feeling I might be doing something that isn't right.

These things make it worse, not better.

I am sorry you are in pain.

Instead, spend some time with yourself. Locate that inner fracture.

Set free this girl you are not in love with so she can go find someone who is, and so you can find yourself.

Anything

The moment you claim something as yours — anything at all — what that means is that you are guaranteed to lose it.

He's Hiding Something

Your partner is hiding something.

Often hiding something is less about deceit and more about privacy. About vital, indispensable personal space.

We all have things to hide. We want to appear better, bigger, more awesome, more virtuous, more talented. Cooler. Edgier. More impressive. Not to others. To ourselves.

We hide things in a (misguided) effort to make others happy, to satisfy something unquenchable, in an attempt to make someone love us more.

To keep someone else from something we did that we wish we could either take back or keep under wraps forever.

We hide things because it's easier.

We hide things because it saves us from giving long, winding explanations.

Explanations are exhausting and, I don't know. I don't know why I did that.

We hide things because we think it's a way to escape the consequences of things we would rather not face.

Everyone is hiding something. I've stopped looking for signs. I've walked away from living a life weighed down by suspicion.

I accept the people I love as fallible and trust them. If they are hiding something, I give them space to do that, because that space is essential.

And, because I'm hiding something too.

If I feel that what they are hiding is too big, too damaging, if it fractures a fundamental, clearly established rule, if I conclude they cannot be trusted, I don't need to discover anything. I don't need to study subtle and less obvious hints. I don't need to catch or outsmart them. I don't need to look through their things in an effort to validate my absence of trust.

What I need to do is leave them.

I have no business keeping close to me someone I don't trust.

Extra Large Fries

My friend's boyfriend wants her to be healthy and strong. He wants her to take care of herself. He watches what she eats, argues with her when she orders fries, glares at her when she reaches out for a piece of chocolate.

When he travels, the first thing she does is go buy a bag of junk food she eats alone in front of the television.

My significant other cannot "make me" do anything, not even in the name of doing so for my own good. That job is already taken — by me. Only I can do that.

What my significant other can do is be the best he can be, which might spark something in me. He can love me. Who he is might very well inspire me.

For another, that's all we can do.

Is It Weird to Kiss With Your Eyes Open?

Each one of your senses is a completely different avenue for sensation and for pleasure.

The person you are kissing can feel good, but why stop there? He can also smell good, sound good, taste good.

Kissing with your eyes open means kissing can also look good.

Sometimes, the involvement of more senses implies more pleasure. Or you can switch a few on and off by touching/not touching, hearing/not hearing, smelling/not smelling, seeing/not seeing.

Many people feel closing your eyes allows you to fully appreciate and feel the other senses. Is this true for you?

There is only one way to find out.

Your senses are designed to take in the world, and for your enjoyment. Playing with them is not weird. It's wonderful.

Why Make Excuses for Him?

Because maybe it's me. Maybe I expect too much.

Because maybe he will feel trapped if I am too demanding.

Because I've never told him what I want.

Because I'm trying to pick my battles.

Because this is not worth the argument.

Because I prefer not to fight.

Because I already know this is who he is.

Because I'm not going to change him.

Because I'm afraid to lose him.

Because I'm afraid to be alone.

Because I don't know what to say.

Because I'm too scared to see he doesn't care enough.

The Real Question

Relationships are hard — really hard.

They are everything — by everything I mean that within your relationships is the meaning of life.

Relationships are full of purpose and of light.

Also, they are drudgery, and often darkness. They can be dramatic and volatile and untenable. And, worse — they can be boring, tedious, make everything feel old. So old.

What makes relationships stick has nothing to do with saccharine tips like "never go to bed angry" or "make sure you respect date night".

It's more about the realization that you are flawed, that the person you are in a relationship with is flawed, that you will not always be happy, will not always feel love, will not always feel like you like or even know this other person very much at all.

Who is this guy, anyway?

But there is something above all this — above you, above me, above love, above us, some obstinate, fundamental thing that against all reason declares *"This is it. Whatever this turns into, I am going to stick it out".*

In other words, relationships that survive decades don't survive because of love or perfection or wonder but because they accepted early on that the dynamic would be replete with ups and downs — and often for years mostly downs.

So sometimes the relationship feels like it's on, so on. And sometimes it's off. And sometimes I don't even know what it is.

It doesn't matter.

The real question is — is this the person you want to stick it through for, or not?

Only you have the answer — what I can tell you is that if she is, the relationship is going to feel "off" a lot.

That's what relationships do.

Fatal Programming

I have a friend who witnessed her Dad beat up her mom regularly.

Today, my friend's husband hits her and she cannot bring herself to leave.

One day she told me that on the weeks he doesn't hit her she feels he doesn't love her anymore.

It's hard to leave because abusive relationships snap perfectly into the way we were originally programmed to define love.

Mars

I was born with an exuberant, compulsive, obsessive, excessive nature.

I pounce on people, like an overstimulated puppy.

All my life I've heard *"Dushka, my god reel it in"*.

I spend most of my energy exercising restraint.

It's exhausting.

Today, if I hear any version of this, such as *"I need space"*, *"back off"*, *"we need to dial this down"*, *"we are going too fast"*, whatever, dude.

I run.

If you want space I will send you to Mars.

Saying anything that sounds like "back off" sticks a finger into a narrative I have suffered from since I was little.

What I need to learn is calibration. *"I need space"* does not mean *"I don't love you"*. It does not mean *"go away forever"*.

It's not an insult. It just means "I need space", something I happen to frequently need myself.

The best solution to this issue, and any issue, is self-awareness. *Hello again, terrifying, primal fear. I see you. I know what you are feeling. You are OK. I like who you are so much, Dushka.*

Please. Don't run. Calibrate.

Not on You

Many people are in terrible, empty relationships and *never* cheat.

Many people are in extremely fortunate, happy relationships, and cheat anyway.

Do you ever wonder how that can be?

The answer is that when someone cheats, it has nothing at all to do with the person they cheated on. Nothing.

It has everything to do with themselves.

If you are cheated on, it's so painful it feels someone has set your insides on fire. They are hurting you, betraying you, failing you, breaking every promise they made.

And yet, cheating is not personal.

A person cheats because of emptiness. Because of despair. Because of hunger. Because of loneliness. Because of insatiability. Because of entitlement. Because of fear. Because of power.

You do not get cheated on because of your shortcomings.

It's easy to attribute the cheating to the partner — because you abandoned me, ignored me, didn't make me happy, didn't give me what I needed — but the partner is never the reason.

If someone cheats on me, it is never ever because I am not enough. Not because I am inadequate. Not because another woman is better than me, more beautiful than me, younger than me, sexier than me.

It is because of a fracture in the cheater.

I know this for sure because I have cheated, and the times I have done so I have done it for reasons unrelated to the man I was with.

I know this because I have been cheated on, and the person who cheated on me went on to cheat on others.

Cheating is on the cheater. It is not on you.

He's Friends With His Ex

Your boyfriend is friends with his ex and this makes you uncomfortable.

Getting along with your exes means you pick people well, you are capable of navigating a relationship healthy enough to evolve, you have learned to fight fair, and managed to come out on the other side with a friendship.

The fact your boyfriend gets along with his ex speaks well of him.

If you decide to let your discomfort dictate your actions, you will ask that he stop seeing her.

If he agrees, you have contributed to the dissolution of an important relationship that has gone through a lot.

But also, you have set forth a course of action that will sooner or later destroy your relationship.

You will become controlling of each other, insecure, demanding that the other do things we should be doing for ourselves: manage our self-doubt, our feelings and our fears.

"You can't see your ex" becomes *"I don't like your friends"* and eventually turns into *"Stay small and circumscribed because you in any way getting out there and expanding, you being loved by anyone at all, will make me feel threatened"*.

Relationships should free you. They should nurture you, make you better people.

They are not supposed to strangle you.

It's easy to take all the work you are supposed to do on yourself and dump it on the other person. It's so easy, but it comes with a price.

What you should do is the difficult thing: acknowledge your discomfort and work through it.

"It's hard that you get along with your ex but this is my issue to work through and not yours. I wanted to tell you about it because I want you to see where I am coming from if I act seemingly irritated or irrational. But, the fact that she's your friend is great, and I want to get myself to a place where I can support anything that's important to you."

That's what love is: to want what is best for the other person, rather than demand the other person make me feel better about the vast array of things I should be learning to be comfortable with.

Here is what happens when you take the easy road: the damn lesson keeps coming back.

Afraid to Lose Him

Feeling afraid to lose someone is very painful. It means I approach the relationship from a place of anxiety and insecurity.

Because it usually results in grasping, it tends to devolve into possessiveness, attempt to control and jealousy.

This fear of losing someone I love tends to not be related to my relationship but rather towards the way I regard myself.

If this continues unaddressed it will present itself in every relationship I have.

This is because the source of the problem is not that I believe you will leave me but that I believe I am not worthy of you staying.

Compatibility/Love

If I loved my partner very much and they told me they wanted to try something — anything at all — I would ask myself if what they wanted to try was compatible with who I am.

Saying yes has nothing to do with making someone happy.

Saying no has nothing to do with wanting to hurt someone.

The question is this: does what you want align with who I am?

Do we want the same things?

If we do not, regardless of the volume and intensity of my love for you, we are not compatible.

If I don't recognize this, we will put each other through hell.

The Right Time to Propose

The Greeks have two words for time.

One is Chronos, chronological time, sequential time. What time is it? What time would you like to meet?

The second is Kairos, the right time, the time to act, propitious time.

Your watch keeps chronos.

Kairos, my friend, is in you.

Old Photos

Boyfriend has a box of photographs that depict his life before my arrival.

Photos with his parents and his two older sisters. Photos with his dad, whom I never got to meet. Photos with old friends and former girlfriends, their long, curly hair and their lanky legs and their school bags.

Photos of his wedding, with his whole family and their friends, everyone dressed up, formal and serious and hopeful and in love.

We are what we have lived. We are our experiences, the people we have come across and those we have loved. We are where we have been. Don't let anyone try to erase that.

Possessive Love

Have you ever seen an insect get tangled up in a spider's web?

It thrashes to set itself free, fights for its life as the spider slowly approaches it.

She watches and begins to cloak the insect in, makes the threads of her sticky web thicker when she ties down the insect's limbs.

Soon the prisoner is motionless.

This is when the spider comes in close and bites the insect, then waits, then bites again.

The spider's venom makes its way through the insect's body, paralyzing it. The insect twitches as the spider feeds on it over several days.

This insect was trapped, immobilized, poisoned and eaten alive.

It would be contrary to nature to assume the insect could ever love the spider.

We can instead expect it to become an empty, bloodless paper shell.

Brutally Honest

Being brutal with a lover is pretty messed up.

You can be absolutely, unflinchingly, directly honest without being brutal.

Honesty is good. "Brutal" honesty is mean spirited, callous, and ugly.

A lot of folks try to justify lying to a partner by blabbing about how they don't want to hurt their partner and brutal honesty is hurtful and yadda yadda yadda, as if the only two choices are "lies" and "brutal honesty."

There's a third choice: compassionate honesty. Be honest while at the same time being considerate, respectful, and compassionate toward your partner.

He's Numb. Do I Stay or Go?

Who are you?

Are you inherently expressive, demonstrative, emphatic, animated?

If you are and struggle to adjust your nature to a person who is numb, if you are always concerned about being perceived as overwhelming or perpetually worried that you — glorious, enthusiastic you — will push him away by virtue of being you, modulating your behavior will be the struggle of your relationship.

Do you want to live constantly exercising restraint?

Do you want to tell someone over and over again that you love him only to elicit silence, even discomfort?

The answer to the question you seek is not in who he is or how to determine how much of you to change.

It's not in how on earth to dispense yourself to the person that you love at the right dosage.

The answer to your question is in you, in who you are, in what you want, and in the joy of not settling until you come across a person who wants exactly what is in your nature to want to give.

I deserve to be in a place where I don't need to second guess things inherent to my nature, and so do you my friend.
So do you.

De-Dramatize

If I am in a relationship and something happens that makes me uncomfortable, I have two choices:

Make it bigger, generating drama.

Make it smaller, put it in its rightful place.

Say my guy is talking to other women.

To make it bigger, I make it about me. I wrap it in my insecurities. I mix it in with an inner narrative guaranteed to make things worse. I spin out. *How disrespectful. How inconsiderate. He shows no regard for my feelings. This is a clear sign he will cheat on me. I will show him.*

By the time I am done talking to myself about this, listening to all my heated thoughts about it, the argument that I take to him has taken on the proportions of a nuclear weapon. The whole relationship is at stake.

To make it smaller, I ask myself — what am I making this mean?

This is very different from "what does this mean?" as it recognizes the role I play in its interpretation.

Then, I untangle it from my own narrative. I spin it down instead of up. *Talking to women is normal, and I know this because I talk to other men. It means nothing. I need to work on this discomfort within myself, because asking him to walk the world with blinders on talking only to people of his gender is not reasonable. It's not healthy.*

I want my relationships to be light, to be easy, and maybe even to shed light on the times I make things bigger than they need to be.

I watch myself closely. I choose to make issues smaller. I shun drama.

Drama is exhausting, it's destructive, and I would rather dedicate my energy to more worthwhile things. Sex, for example, is way more fun.

Vulnerable

Love. It lays us bare. It splits us open. It strips us of every defense.

Look at me standing before you. You could take it all.

What this means, unfortunately, is that the other person can hurt me even when it's the last thing they'd want.

In other words, it's not that you are armed — it's that I am vulnerable.

What I do is assume good intent. I assume you are doing your best. I assume you would never hurt me intentionally.

I assume clumsiness will get better.

But mostly, feeling insulted, wronged or indignant is not constructive.

To give us a fighting chance I assume you are not perfect. I assume you are fallible. This fallibility makes any transgression easier to understand and therefore easier to forgive.

Now, are you hurting me intentionally? Are you trespassing on boundaries I have made clear? Are you breaking the rules of our relationship? Are you cruel?

Then I pack it up. There is nothing else to do here.

I'm Sorry

At first glance I worry apologizing makes me feel weak and disempowered, but look at it: it's just the opposite.

"I am so sorry I did that" makes me feel expansive, generous — rather than tight, coiled, small, petty.

It pushes something hard and painful, like a rock in my shoe, clear out of the way.

Stepping out of my indignant thoughts — which make my brain increasingly heated — and putting myself in the other person's shoes grants me compassion. This is the antidote to anger. It is like air conditioning, cool and fresh, for the insides of my head.

When I apologize, I have my eyes set on the relationship — wide, broad, open — and not on the infraction — narrow, shallow, shortsighted.

An apology doesn't mean "I am diminished" but rather "I didn't mean to hurt you."

It's for all these reasons that I try to be the one to apologize first.

Why Do We Ignore Red Flags and Get Married Anyway?

Because I have no idea what to do with my life.

Because I want to be married.

Because I don't want to be single.

Because I need to get on with my life.

Because it's time to grow up.

Because this is what I'm supposed to do.

Because this is what everyone else does.

Because marriage will save me from breaking up.

Because marriage will save me from myself.

Because if I am married my life won't feel empty.

Because I want others to see I did it: marriage is a form of success.

Because I don't love him but he checks all the boxes.

Because many things aren't working but I know I can change him.

Because I will learn to love him.

Because marriage demonstrates commitment.

Because I'm pregnant.

Because if I don't get pregnant I will miss out on having kids.

Because marriage will force us to work out whatever we can't work out now.

Give Me

Do you know what I want? I want the ability to drop all of my demands on others.

I annoy myself, frustrate myself, hurt myself when I place at the center of my perception all the things that I want that I am not getting.

It feels like someone placed something delicate on the palm of my hand and I am squeezing, constricting, my jaws clenched, every bit of me grabbing, grasping.

If only you could be. Change that. Do this. Give me. Give me.

Give me.

It's so draining to find fault with everything, to be relentless with my complaints and expectations.

I would much rather exist in liquid, relaxed, generous suspension. Love makes me feel abundant, expansive and whole and if this is what you make me feel, then you already give me all I need.

I don't care. I don't care about the things you should be doing, the flowers you are not bringing, the dinners you don't take me to, the times we are not slow dancing, the birthdays and anniversaries that keep coming and you keep forgetting.

Instead, surprise me. Let me be grateful for whatever you already are.

This is not something I want for you. I don't want it so I can love better.

I want it because life is short and the last thing I want is to have to live with me when I exhaust me.

Stronger

If someone is cruel, abusive or deliberately hurtful, that's a person I make an effort to stay away from.

But if I have a loving, long term relationship and in the day in, day out fallibility, turbulence and tousle he says something that causes me pain, I try to be generous.

This means that instead of telling myself *"Wow, what he said is unforgivable, how dare he, how could he"* instead I say *"I know you are hurt Dushka, but also you know he didn't mean that".*

Instead of saying *"I just cannot, should not tolerate these things"* I instead say *"Dushka, be fair. You were fighting and you said some hurtful things too".*

Instead of saying *"This is not something you come back from, things will never be the same, this will forever burn a hole in my heart"* I get off the high horse of my indignation and say *"I forgive you. I forgive you because the fact that you are my person matters more than a fleeting, heated argument. And because forgiving you feels much better than being furious at you".*

Then instead of saying *"Something here was irreparably broken, shattered"* I say *"Hey, we learned a lot from this — in the future we will fight better, to build, not to tear down, to fix, not to wound".*

Then we see we have grown and feel good that we took this hurtful thing and let it make us stronger, instead of amplifying it and letting it destroy us.

Mercury

Have you ever held mercury in the palm of your hand?

(I have, before I knew it was dangerous to do so — so please consider this the metaphor that it is without trying this at home.)

Mercury is a liquid metal and if you hold your hand open it pools in the center of it, shiny, metallic, cool, peaceful, still, alive.

If you squeeze your hand shut it squirts out through your fingers.

Mercury can only be held loosely, in a palm wide open, and I think the same is true for love.

Needy love is desperate, voracious, possessive, jealous, grasping. Your heart, filled with fear and an illusion of dependency, loops tightly around it, ultimately squeezing out anything beautiful.

Needy love means you will (sooner or later) lose everything.

It's best to love without needing. This is healthy love, open love, airy love, the kind that sets you free.

If I am insecure I want people to need me. Because if there is no "need", why else would they stay?

Insecurity does not let me see that the reason to stay is me; just me — not what I do, what I solve or what I provide.

This is how I become attracted only to people with a tendency to suffocate me with the kind of love that needs.

Healthy/Toxic

Do you think this person has your back? Or can you never count on him?

Do you talk or are you afraid to?

Do you feel buoyed after a tough conversation or completely depleted, drained, exhausted? (Watch your energy levels around this person. They reveal a lot.)

Do you feel you trust despite difficulties, or are you full of suspicion even when things are going smoothly?

Do you feel safe or in danger, vulnerable, at risk?

Do you feel seen, loved, or diminished, belittled?

Is the relationship tough but fundamentally stable or volatile and full of constant drama?

Are you true to yourself or does the approval of the other person take precedence?

Are you clear on how far you are willing to go or is what you are willing to do a moving target you have maybe lost track of?

Remember when you said it would never be OK to be yelled at?

Does this person make you want to be better or bring out your worst possible side? Look. Look at who you have become.

The first is a healthy relationship. The second is a toxic one.

Communication

Have you ever encountered someone and thought *"I want him in my life"*?

I'm not necessarily referring to a romantic connection — although I'm not excluding that.

I mean a clear, powerful, life-directing *"You. I want more of you"*.

That's what I felt the instant I met him. Every time I got to talk to him, despite not knowing him, despite conversations in fits and starts, the feeling grew.

I found him massively exotic — in every way different from me, quirky and surprising — a tangle, avid and intricate and meticulous and sweet.

During one of our intent chats, (he expresses himself in a cocktail of unclear/lucid spurts) he revealed how complex his personal life was.

I listened, then made a mental note to always talk to him about the things I felt connected us — creativity, hunger, restlessness, fantasy — but to never talk to him about my day in, day out struggles.

The last thing I wanted was become yet another thing that burdened him. What I wanted was to provide, if only for a moment, a respite, breathing space, deliverance.

To me, the best friends grant you precisely what you lack.

A few months later something truly awful happened in my life. He — on sheer impulse, on instinct — was the first person I thought to call. I felt powerless and desperate and completely alone and knew that in his gentle voice I'd find a measure of solace.

I did not call him. I had promised myself I wouldn't. I was worried he would feel devoid of recourse. There was nothing he could do for me, and feeling like there was nothing he could do was precisely the sensation that I wanted to spare him.

It was a couple of months after that decision that we had a strained encounter. We weren't angry or even distant. Just not smooth. Not easy.

"You know what I would like to see some day, Dushka?" he said. *"I want to see you share more of your life with me. You are so reserved — I find out about things about you through other people. I think the next big step in this friendship of ours is for you to think of reaching out to me if you need someone to talk to."*

Without communication, you have people who badly want the very same thing yet stay away from it, based on the silent assumptions we all make.

We try, you see. We try to be good, to take care of the people that we love. It's just that without communication, we can't possibly know what that really is.

Breaking Up and the Aftermath

The First Heartbreak

The first time I experienced the initial symptoms of a break up I didn't know what was happening to me.

I felt brokenhearted and anxious, wanted something to go back to the way it was but couldn't articulate that I instead wanted everything to go back to what I had once imagined it would be.

Everything was displaced. Everything. I couldn't sleep. I couldn't eat. Even the clothes in my closet felt like they had been selected for somebody else. I needed a change. I got a haircut.

Who was this person I was becoming?

I felt sorrow and a sense of not being tethered to anything but also like I was breaking out of a confined space into a wider — if frightening — world.

I felt certain — certain — that my life was falling apart, that I would never find anyone else and that I was through with love.

Now a breakup hurts just as much but I know no one decides what it's going to be like but me.

We are going to be friends because we know each other and have invested a huge amount of time into each other and that to me is not worth throwing out.

Nothing is lost — things are in flux, in transformation. It's painful but it happens because it's necessary for our own evolution.

I am free, and so are you. Regardless of how this feels, the truth is my life is far from over.

I get a new haircut and an orange dress and know, because I've done this before, that my life is just beginning.

Enough

The worst relationship I ever had was intense, controlling, and a tangle of emotions so enormous it quickly became beyond my ability to manage.

The intense, controlling, emotionally unmanageable one was me.

In the aftermath of the breakup I felt abandoned, indignant, wronged, tragically misunderstood and betrayed.

That was a walk in the park compared to what came next.

The difficult part was the realization that what made me love and admire him even more was his decision to leave me.

This sums up one of my most painful breakups: layering on top of genuine heartbreak the fact that I was the bad guy and that the ex had been right to run.

It was at this point that I realized I'd had enough.

What He Deserves

If I have a boyfriend I don't love, this does not make me the bad guy. I don't govern my heart: she falls in love with people she is not supposed to, and refuses to love perfectly good men.

What this boyfriend who loves me deserves — as soon as possible — is the truth. I have to tell him that he is wonderful and kind and that I don't love him.

That the fact I don't love him has nothing to do with him.

I need to tell him that what I want for him is his happiness, and that I wish he can quickly find what he deserves: someone he loves and who loves him back as fully and as well as he loves me.

Little Things

Maybe when you are with friends he says things that very subtly undermine you when instead you want to feel buoyed by the person you love.

Or he'll bug you and say he's just teasing but hurt you with his tendency to find your irritation amusing.

Or he will not offer to drive you home or give you his sweater when it's cold and you can't help but interpret these admittedly small things as symptoms of an absence of interest.

Or he in turn will interpret genuine concern (did you make a doctor's appointment?) for you trying to control him.

Maybe something in your character makes things that should be very simple incredibly complicated. You want to plan ahead for the week so you can spend time together and he, well. He's not a planner.

Or he will want you to be someone other than who you are. And at first you try but eventually you being exhausted crowds out you being in love.

I'd rather miss you than be someone I'm not.

You will write him a poem and he will read it and ask you to explain it to him.

Or, you write and he doesn't read what you write. And it matters because this is not you writing. It's who you are.

Untenable

I grew up in a macho society where women were regarded as property.

My environment was all I knew and within it I belonged to the guy I was with. I found him saying I was his both protective and flattering.

Tragically, I do not have a submissive personality. I have always been headstrong, independent and opinionated.

Against social norms it made sense to me to be my own person. I lashed out when someone tried to control me, forbid something or tell me what to do.

At the same time, dating someone who didn't want me to be his felt like he did not love me.

This catch-22 was invisible to me and I could not understand why my relationships were so dysfunctional.

Later I understood, but still did not know how to change what I felt.

Why was the guy I was dating not checking up on me? Why did he let me have male friends? Why did my revealing outfit not outrage him?

I had to open my eyes and talk myself into healthy relationships, repeat to myself that just because he wasn't acting crazed with jealousy, just because he wasn't telling me what to do, just because he wasn't expecting me to serve him did not mean he didn't love me.

This is where I come from. From this place I can say for certain that love is not possessive. If someone loves you they want you to be happy, even if it means being without you.

I understand how this can feel unsafe, untethered, as if you were suddenly released from a secure hold, becoming unmoored. But once you see, you cannot unsee it. What was once your reality becomes irrational, untenable.

If you work at it your patterns will become detectable, eventually untangle, to be healthy and free.

Walk Away

When I dread instead of look forward to seeing you.

When I feel perpetually exhausted.

When nothing seems to get resolved without high-octane drama.

When the reasons for the relationship are internal. It's not that I love you, it's that I'm lonely.

When what you think I mean is not at all what I said, and this happens systematically.

Or when you say that's not what you said, and I know that you did, and this happens systematically.

When you mistreat me: raise your voice, gaslight me, play games, twist words.

When we want different things.

When despite our efforts, we are fundamentally incompatible.

When there is an absence of trust.

When anything in our dynamic is hurting either your life or mine. In particular when what I want is for your life to be better — which is what I always want.

When my life is not interesting to you — or yours to me.

When I don't like who I am when I am with you.

When the only time we truly connect is when we have sex. And that's great but I want connection everywhere. Everywhere.

When the most you can give me is less than what I need.

After you've clearly stated that you cannot love me.
(I understand.)

How to Make a Breakup Easier

Let me tell you something about breakups: you can design your own.

The general expectation is drama. Pain. Fighting. *How could you do this to me? How is it possible that I didn't ever see this side of you? I want to hurt you. I don't want you to be happy.* We will do things to each other out of spite.

But what if you are both wonderful people and love each other and are just not compatible? What if I am capable of seeing that it's not that you are trying to make things difficult for me but rather that you cannot help being the (really quite wonderful) person that you are?

Then what you've got is someone you truly love, and truly like, that just can't be your significant other. You instead have a friend who feels like family, who really knows you, who has been with you through thick and thin.

Why would you want to throw out someone like that? To put yourself in a situation where they go from being central to your life to never seeing him again?

This makes no sense to me.

So design your own breakup. You two decide how it's going to be. Look, we are going to do this differently. We will watch over each other, keep our eye on what really matters: us. Our very particular relationship. (*Please — keep the coffee table and the bed.*)

Let's take our time and help each other get settled into a new place. Let's make this as painless as possible. *Do you miss me? Just call me. I really want to see that new movie with you anyway.*

Did you meet someone else? Of course it's going to be hard but I will work through it because I would love to meet her. And tell me. Does she know how lucky she is?

I am not suggesting this process is easy. Feelings get in the way, and ego and pettiness and unfairness and indignation.

Remember every day to keep your eye on the most important thing.

Necessary Light

I was married for 15 years and for 13 of those years I was very happy.

In the last two something began to happen to my relationship that was so disconcerting I could not articulate it.

I didn't tell a soul because talking about it felt like an act of treason, like I was revealing the details of something intimate and sacred.

I was surrounded by friends, and at the same time completely alone.

This total isolation was something I did to myself.

I struggled through the decomposition of my relationship and subsequent divorce all on my own and didn't talk about it for many years.

Today I talk about my relationships. I carefully consider how I am representing things, and never cast someone I love in a negative light. But I have discovered that talking to others about what happens in my life is indispensable and fills dark spaces with necessary light.

Leave Me Here

I have always been deeply affected by break ups, even when I break up with someone I don't love anymore. I feel like someone tied me to the back of a wagon and dragged me across the desert. Please just leave me here. I feel bereft, devastated. Everything hurts.

I question if my life is worth living.

You know what I feel? Like every one of my cells is held together by a special glue that suddenly doesn't work anymore. I feel like I come undone, like I can't keep myself together. I function, but barely. I hide in the bathroom (or under my desk) and cry.

I have many, many internal fractures I have been working on through the years. One of my biggest is figuring out what it is about the end of a relationship that destroys me to the degree that it does, in particular when I am so fiercely independent, when I love being alone so much and value my sovereignty more than anything.

As I work through what the heck goes on in my fragile (or maybe indestructible) heart, I think of Rumi, who assures me *"the cure from the pain is in the pain"* and that *"Look, Dushka* (I imagine him saying my name), *you have to keep breaking your heart until it opens."*

Oh, Rumi.

Sigh.

Also, I write about the things I learn along the way, and the steps I take to recover. Then I share them to hopefully make things a bit easier for anyone who reads them.

You know what? After a breakup I always, always end up in a better place.

It's just torture to get there.

How Was Your Heart Broken?

I wanted him to be something he wasn't.

I wanted him to say something he wouldn't.

I wanted him to do something he didn't.

It all comes back to my expectations.

I break my own heart.

Sure I Can

If a relationship is not good for me, I don't wait until I'm no longer in love to leave.

I leave even if I still love him.

I don't leave because I don't love you anymore. I leave because I love myself.

As such, "being too in love" is not a valid reason to stay in a relationship that's bad for me.

"I can't leave" is just not true.

It's so easy to say *"I can't, I can't, I just can't oh my god I love him so"*.

But, watch me.

Sure I can.

The reason I stay is usually because I am scared. *Because, what if I regret this? Because I would rather be in a bad relationship than alone. Because, what if this is as good as it gets? Because, what if it gets better?*

Because, I lack faith in myself.

Staying in a relationship that is bad for me negatively affects me by continuing to undermine my faith in myself.

In other words, the longer I stay, the harder it is to leave.

The way out is to leave. Now. Right now.

I am so in love, and I think I will love you for a long time.

I'm going to leave you anyway.

This is absolutely terrifying.

I leave, and it's hard. Really hard. It hurts. I rebuild myself. I slowly recover. I slowly collect all the things I had lost. And one day, not too far away from today, I wonder what the heck took me so long.

All these things are true for you too.

Not a Matter of Time

If I was ready to settle down and he was not, I would conclude that he and I want different things and as such are not compatible.

As hard as this is to take in, the fact is this: wanting different things is seldom a matter of time.

Me being ready to settle down and him not being ready means that either he will never be ready or he will be ready to settle down, just not with me.

"Waiting" for someone to want what they don't want right now has a tendency to result in me becoming someone I don't like. In me being a nag, and bitter, and with constant, low grade pain and anger. In me exerting pressure and expressing impatience and dissatisfaction.

It results in him feeling inadequate and like he's constantly falling short and unable to make me happy. In him postponing the inevitable, which is to tell me straight up that he does not want what I want.

Or, it results in him feeling forced into something he didn't want, which does not leave the relationship in a good place. *Because look, this is not what I wanted and you pushed and now look at us, trapped here.*

I would keep this man in my life as a good friend, but not as a significant other.

Open to Change

If you and another person are "incompatible" it means you cannot happily live together.

It does not mean you are not "open to change" or that you "are not willing to put in the work".

It often means you are absolutely, intensely wanting, fighting, struggling to make it work — all you want is for this to just work — but you cannot get there from here.

Relinquishing a characteristic that makes you incompatible feels like you are compromising not just your happiness but your identity.

If one of you is punctual and the other always late, you can negotiate a somewhat incongruous life with its own brand of rhythm.

But what if one of you is monogamous and the other polyamorous? What if one of you places a great deal of importance in material things and the other does not assign meaning to money? What if one is a systematic liar and the other requires honesty in order to function? What if one is deeply insecure and the other repeatedly hurt by being constantly doubted?

Is changing to meet your relationship's demands making you a better person? Is it stretching you, contributing to your growth?

Or is it forcing you to be someone other than who you are?

Don't believe "love conquers all." It does not.

Unconditional Love

Unconditional means categorical, absolute, without boundaries, reservations or conditions. It means definite, no holds barred, unqualified.

Unconditional love sounds whole, complete, but let's take a closer look.

If I love someone unconditionally can they hurt me, then do so again and again? Can they be violent? Can they treat me without regard or respect? Can they limit me, restrict me, wrong me, assault me?

If they do all these things, must I still love them?

Unconditional love is not a healthy vow to make. It desecrates my love for myself. I love, but that love cannot be lied to, betrayed, abused.

I do not practice unconditional love.

My love cannot be ill treated, or you will lose it forever.

His Way

I briefly dated a guy who made fun of me, privately and in front of others. When I told him it hurt my feelings he requested that I lighten up. This was "his way."

The fact that his way was intractable and involved knowingly being hurtful to others revealed we were incompatible.

I want the people closest to me to be honest, direct, loving and supportive and have decided that this, far from unreasonable, should be a minimum requirement.

Never Again

I cannot leave what I have now, even if it is unsatisfactory, because I will never _____ again:

I can't break up with a person that I love but who is not good for me because I will never love again.

I can't leave my current relationship even if it's unsatisfactory because I will never meet anyone else again.

I can't leave my current job even if it's unsatisfactory because I will never be employed again.

Every single time I have allowed this "never again" fear to delay and paralyze me I have done so because it disguises itself as my voice of reason and I feel remaining trapped is the responsible choice.

Every single time I take an enormous leap of faith and decide to "act irrationally", to "do something crazy" I prove that what kept me paralyzed was a lie.

With one life to live what is irrational is the assumption that remaining stuck will keep me safe.

"I will never again" is a master of disguise. She is an impostor.

How to Recover From Heartbreak

Heartbreak is incredibly painful. It hurts so much I feel like I'm dying. Or, like I want to.

Here are the steps I follow to return to the world of the living.

I hold on. The first thing I do is remind myself that my feelings are temporary. As surely as this *feels* like there will never again be light, the fact is it will pass. As impossible as this seems right now, I will get better. Everything will get better.

Hold on. Just hold on.

I assure myself that some day this will matter a lot less. Every one of the thoughts that are unbearable right now will not be unbearable later. *He will find someone else. He will love someone else.* This will one day not matter.

I remind myself that not being loved and my self worth are not related. Someone not loving me — even someone who once loved me and who now doesn't love me anymore — has nothing to do with me. Wonderful people are dumped every day. I myself have stopped loving really, really good guys. I am worth loving and what I am going through right now does not indicate that I am not. Associating the two is a fallacy.

I identify what I miss. Sure I miss him. But I also miss being in a relationship. A lot of what I lost is the part of me that he brought out — who I was when I was with him. I don't need him for that. Who was she, this person that I was? What do I need to do to bring her back?

I set aside all skepticism and doubt. *Was what we had ever real? Did he ever love me? Was this all a lie?* All these questions are useless, self destructive and torturous and I am in enough pain. This is enough pain. I don't invite any more.

I reject anything that will keep me tied to feeling like this. The sense that he wronged me, that I hate him, that I have to get back at him so he can pay for what he's done. I want to get better. I want to move on and all these feelings are nothing but shackles.

I exercise. The very last thing I want is to move. I don't want to step outside. I don't want to stretch or run or be out of breath or break a sweat. I do it anyway.

I stay in the present. Right now I am here with me and I love me. In the past he broke my heart and in the future he will be with someone else and — right here. Right here with me is where it's at. We will get better if for now we stick to right here, right now.

I throw out any negative talk. *You are worthless, unlovable, this was your fault and you are terrible at relationships.* Oh, yeah? I am handling as much as I can right now so all you absurd, inaccurate, depressive, negative lies can go wait outside.

I surround myself with love. I spend time with my family and friends and rather than fill their ears with the calamitous state of my love life I ask them to list out my qualities. Maybe list them out more than once. Remind me. Remind me why you love me.

I get someone to touch me. When I am in a relationship I hold hands, I hug, I snuggle. A broken heart makes me feel I ache for that. I ask my friends to hug me. I physically lean on them. I go get a massage. For me, touch deprivation is a thing.

I get out of my head. Honestly, I am so very tired of me. I ask my friends to give me a rest from myself and to instead talk about them. I find someone who could use my help. I volunteer. One day I spent a whole day at an animal shelter petting and holding puppies. I forgot about me for a while.

I make a list of things I neglected to make room for my relationship. I love to read and now I have time. I love to spend the day alone and wander. I love poetry readings and swimming. I love rock climbing and learning new things.

I make a list of things I have always wanted to do. I want to go to Savannah, Georgia. I have never been to New Zealand. I want to see the Northern Lights. I want to learn how to make macarons. Or maybe I just want to go to a macaron making class so I can meet other people interested in making macarons.

I remind myself that love is a privilege. That I want to love well. That the only way to get good at this is to practice, and get my heart broken, and recover, and try again.

How to Cope With His Departure

I know you don't believe me now (and good for you) but feelings are just feelings.

By this I mean that they are fleeting, and that the feeling that you think contains you, defines you, guides you, will one day, possibly soon, no longer exist.

You will love someone else one day, maybe more than this person you are now lamenting you will never be with.

And this new love will be more complete and more fortunate because being together will happen with ease, with grace, will happen now, right now instead of never.

And you will look back and wonder how it was that you were so certain your happiness was so tangled up in this person that you haven't even thought about in years.

I wonder what became of him? I wonder how he is doing?

I had no way of knowing this then but wow. What a stroke of incredible good fortune that things did not work out for us.

And that is how you cope.

Northern Lights

I don't believe in marriage.

There is no happily ever after.

Let me tell you what happens instead of you riding off into the sunset. You lose touch with yourself. Where do you go? Where are those interests you said you would not neglect?

What happened to that trip you'd take to see the Northern Lights?

You get married in large part because you believe marriage will save you. There I was, my long white dress slung over the chair near the bed, and I still had my expectations, my demands, my internal fractures and my perhaps incorrigible hunger for novelty.

Did you know you cannot avoid disappointing me?

That I cannot avoid disappointing you?

Disappointment is insidious and I didn't realize its burden is on me. Because, whose fault is it, if I am the one who has not yet learned to manage the unrealistic things I expect from others? Whose fault is it, if you love me your way instead of loving me the way I want you to?

Who is this objectively beautiful man in my bed? We marry a stranger. It's not that I know him. It's that my imagination has filled in the blanks.

Let me tell you now he doesn't even own the horse he is supposed to come to your rescue on.

Everything — you, him, life, the position of the planets, the patterns of the stars and what you like for breakfast — is ever changing, fluid, mercurial and unsettled.

I promised nothing would change and I did. I'm sorry I did but look around. So did everything else.

You are told you want certain things and by the time you realize you really don't he already gave them to you and there you are, wishing you could return the ring you never use.

I can't promise I won't get married again. This is because when I am infatuated I can't see straight and make promises I already know I can't keep.

I want to give you forever. It's just that I don't really know what that means.

Is Stalking Love?

No.

If I say *"I don't think we should see each other anymore"* or *"this relationship isn't working"* and the other person's reaction is to text or call me multiple times, to "coincidentally" appear in places I frequent, to know where I am or where I'm going to be in some way other than me directly disclosing this information, that's not love. It cannot be considered love. It's creepy, and it's creepy because it is unwanted.

If someone moves on and says they don't want to see me, stalking them ignores everything they have told me. It means I am overriding boundaries and ignoring limits, which, beyond disrespectful, is controlling and more about obsession than about love.

Not Interested

If your boyfriend is not interested in you anymore, this does not mean you are not interesting.

If he doesn't love you, it doesn't mean you are not worth loving.

This is a lesson of self love.

Separate. Separate the feelings of another person from your identity. They are not related.

Learn. Learn that even if someone who matters to you has decided you don't matter to them, you should still be loved, and loved well.

Want. Want nothing less than to be loved well.

How Do I Stop Loving Someone Who Hurts Me?

You don't.

You resolve that your feelings don't get to dictate your actions.

That love makes you powerful rather than weak.

This feeling will teach me and help me grow but I won't let it hurt me.

You are not good for me, so I love you but I choose not to be with you.

Love is a feeling you can carry in your heart as long as it wants to stay there. It's not a primal command.

Don't Fight for Him

I used to expend a huge amount of effort to make time for friends who did not seem to care as much to make time for me.

If a significant other said he didn't want to be with me anymore I thought the solution was to "fight for him" or to "give him space".

What did I need to do to make sure he would come back?

Then I realized it was depleting my soul to strategize ways to be with anyone who did not want to be with me.

It was painful and freeing to see that if someone wanted to be in my life their effort would be proportionate to my own: not at all in a "keeping tabs" sense, but rather as an observer of the natural course that relationships take.

My relationships have improved dramatically now that I only share my time with people who really, really want to share their time with me.

This is the best thing I ever did for myself. I stopped striving for anyone who clearly was not striving for me.

Brave Thing

I can't tell you how far away I was from being interested in a relationship. Or, any form of commitment. Or, any version of an entanglement.

After years of jumping from one relationship to another I was finally free. I had no interest in sharing a life I had just found.

When he told me — very directly — that he was interested in me, my answer was that from every possible angle it was a terrible idea.

I walked away.

The very first time I felt his body against mine what I blurted out was *"I am in so much trouble".*

After that, what I told myself was that this was an anomaly I could manage. If I didn't get attached. If I didn't get involved. If I kept things under control.

How hard could it be? I didn't want any of the things he couldn't offer me.

But then I thought of him all the time.

What was I supposed to do with all this thinking?

I had many other things going on — a full life — yet his existence began to feel like an unintended center of gravity.

How? How, if the center of gravity was me?

I had to learn every day how to hold things loosely. How to love something that would never be mine — not just because it couldn't, but because I didn't want it to be.

I had to learn how to carry things around that I wanted to say but never got a chance to. I'd make notes only to find them obsolete a day or two later.

In my dreams I would walk into dark, empty rooms littered with crumpled sheets of white lined paper.

I had to learn how to stop being so afraid.

If I could go back and change the course of that no name thing I would not.

Most of all because opening myself up to that experience with earnestness, with my whole heart, expressing what I was feeling as clearly as I knew how, was one of the bravest things I'd ever done.

What I do want to say is that if you ever tell yourself *"we can be friends with benefits and not love"*, or *"we can see other people but not get attached"*, or *"I can take part in this without getting emotionally involved"* I would tell you this: be careful.

Be careful, because the fact is our hearts are not governable.

What Can't You Quit?

Him.

I have a hard time quitting him.

It's just that he smells so good.

If my heart decides she loves a guy I have a hard time washing him out of my hair.

My brain is smart and clear.

Dushka. There is nowhere to go from here. He is not good for you. Or, *look he doesn't love you back.* Or, *what are you doing? You don't truly love him — you just think you do.*

God knows why you got yourself into this predicament.

Or *come on — he belongs to someone else and you and I need to move on. Both for us and for him.*

I know I have to and I know I should and I can't quit you. I can't.

Because, I love you.

This is when my head comes in and shakes some sense into my heart.

Dude. Of course you can. It's easy to say you can't but don't you remember all those years before you even knew him? Did you have a hard time surviving without him then?

You did fine and you will again.

And, you don't quit someone because you don't love him.

You quit because you know this does not end well, and you love yourself.

Nothing Is Mandatory

A few years ago I met a guy I thought was terrific. We dated and about five months later he asked me to move in with him. I really didn't want to.

What I want to underline here is that I liked him. I was in fact in love with him. I saw a future with him. I just didn't want to move in with him. The main reason was me — my need for space and my idiosyncratic lifestyle and the fact that I need silence and time with myself.

He felt me turning him down was because I wasn't serious about us.

We continued with this tug, this push-pull, for almost a year. One day he told me that if we didn't move in together the relationship wasn't really progressing. *"I don't want to date you,"* he said. *"I want to live with you."*

We moved in.

I instantly knew I had made a mistake. I loved him so much, but we were very different. Living together put a strain on our relationship. I dealt with friction every day. It was exhausting, and it eventually cost us the relationship.

I have no regrets. He changed my life. I learned so much within the pain of dealing with incompatibility. But, I do wonder if maybe we should have reached another arrangement.

Why is moving in together mandatory? Why couldn't we have been more creative, coming up with something designed for us, instead of falling into what "everyone" does?

Also, the decisions people make are not a measure of their commitment, and certainly not a way to determine our own worth.

More often than not the decisions people make have nothing to do with us.

This knowledge makes whatever happens next a lot easier, as conversations won't be tangled up in the wrong things.

On-and-Off Relationships

In my early twenties I had one relationship that was on, again/off, again.

The first time we broke up we did so because we wanted different things, but we loved each other so kept finding our way to getting back together.

Each time, we'd find that the reasons for our first break up were still there.

Falling back into a relationship is easy: this is a person I already know I am attracted to and already know I like. But, if I have not changed in any fundamental way and he has not changed in any fundamental way, chances are things will play out exactly the way they did the first time.

My on, again/off, again relationship was painful. It was like a movie I had already seen but couldn't stop replaying.

Replaying the movie does not change the way it ends.

The dynamic was unhealthy and disruptive to my life and his but also to our friends and the people around us.

I have no general thoughts about on-and-off relationships because everyone is different, but I can tell you they are not for me.

A System

Toxicity is a dance. It's a system. It's you and me, the way we trigger each other, the action-reaction we elicit in one another. Sure, some people are toxic all on their own. But usually it's the relationship, the dynamic, and as such I play a role.

If I don't see this, if I blame the other person, I condemn myself to repeating this pattern over and over and wondering why on earth every friend/partner/lover I have ends up being bad for me.

Removing someone toxic from my life hurts. In the end it feels like loss, and like failure. *I am losing you, and I thought I could work this out and I couldn't. I did my best and still came up short.*

But also this removal of another person from my life is just the beginning. The real work is that it demands I take a good hard look at what it is that I do so I can hope someday to stop hurting myself.

Finite

At some point along the way we determined that the only measure of success in a relationship is "forever", even though forever is not the case for most relationships, even though many, many connections that don't last very long are wonderful, contribute in indispensable ways to our evolution, make us better people, alter the course of our lives.

I would not be the person I am if it wasn't for you.

My favorite break up story is this: nothing "went wrong". Your relationship did not fail. You did not fail.

Things — special things, priceless things — are finite. They run their course.

The fact that something is ephemeral* does not make it less important, less precious, less meaningful or less of a resounding success.

*Everything. Everything is ephemeral.

Things I Practice

I have two confessions to make.

The first: my love is possessive.

I want what I love (or what I like, appreciate, am interested in, or lust for) to belong to me.

Where I come from this is culturally acceptable, even expected (which is at least part of why I am programmed in this way), and "normal".

But just because something is normal doesn't mean it's healthy, and wanting to possess what I love is not good.

I know this because it makes me suffer.

When what I love displays symptoms of not being mine, (which is inevitable, as you can't own another person) it hurts. A lot.

But if what I love allows itself to be possessed, this is worse, as I end up in a dynamic that inevitably becomes unhealthy.

The first thing I am practicing today, and that I practice every day, like a life sentence, like a mantra, like an incantation: everything I love is free.

To tell you about the second confession, I have to give you a bit of context.

The relationships I am used to — with lovers, with friends, with family — are full contact. I have a small inner circle of friends and we text, call, see each other frequently.

If you are in my life and important to me, I will be within your reach, in attendance, accounted for, present.

I was married to a man I used to work with. We were together all the time and when we weren't we checked in. *Good morning.* Then, *how is your day going? Tell me all about your day.* And, *good night.*

Boyfriend is not like this. It's not that he's not like this with me — it's that his brain doesn't work this way. He's more in his brain, doesn't need touch points, doesn't feel it's necessary to find out how my day is going.

If I say *"tell me all about your day, in chronological order so I don't miss anything!"* he will look alarmed and roll his eyes.

If I travel (which lately I do a lot for work) I might not hear from him for several days.

My second confession is that I forget people don't love me the way I want them to love me. They love me the way they love.

This is the second thing I am practicing today, and that I practice every day.

Accept. Accept that people love you the way they love you. People don't love you the way you want. They love you the way they can.

Confirmation

So, how does it feel to let go of a toxic relationship?

So many feelings, more or less in the following order: exhaustion, emptiness, sadness, a vast sense of loss, a wash of relief, expansion, space, a lightness, happiness.

Yes.

I might sometimes miss you, but I have confirmed what I suspected.

My life is better without you in it.

The Worst

My worst romantic experiences have to do with my own overactive imagination.

Seeing someone from afar and feeling a flash of life in my chest like someone just shook me awake from a dream I had not realized was boring.

Spinning stories that suddenly convince me something exists where in fact nothing has happened.

The assumption that just because I feel something then naturally he does too.

Wanting so desperately to show myself to him. *Look, look. Look at who I am. Get to know me.*

Proceeding to feel crushingly disappointed: at him not being who I fantasized about, him not feeling anything.

I thought I knew you. It felt so real. Why don't you love me? I thought there would be something here.

I break my own heart.

How Could He Throw Me Away?

I don't think it's possible for you to be thrown away.

I think it can certainly *feel* like you were thrown away, and while that feeling is powerful and heartbreaking, these two things are not the same.

Making a distinction between what you feel and what is actually happening is the path to mend your heart.

You cannot be thrown away because you are human and as such you are not disposable.

You're Moving On

Heartbreak is so very painful. It's so painful that you miss what your body and your brain are doing while you are busy suffering.

Your mind is processing.

While you try hard and it feels like you are making no progress, you are mending all the cracks that now feel like inner canyons.

While you try to forget and wonder why you can't, a part of you is slowly, imperceptibly detaching.

You cry, and it's the crying, you see? Crying is essential to healing.

While you wonder how to focus on your life you are focusing on your life.

You are giving yourself the time you need to recover.

What you don't know, because it's hard to see when you're in pain, is that even as you read this you are also moving on.

Does Revenge Cure a Broken Heart?

Revenge keeps your attention pinned on what you believe was done to wrong you instead of allowing you to mourn and move on.

It focuses you on the infraction instead of the love.

It deludes you into believing that if you could get even you would be happy.

It pushes you into doing something — into being someone — you have a high chance of regretting.

Heartbreak, in my experience, is not "curable". Your heart never sets in the same way again, which is precisely what makes it more open.

Heartbreak is how you learn to love better.

Revenge turns a wound designed to expand you into one that festers, poisoning your blood.

It's the difference between a fracture and an infection.

The road to health is healing, harmonious, restoring, soothing, elucidating. Revenge is malignant and venomous and as such cannot be a cure.

I Hope We Get Back Together

Hope is a sense that somehow things will turn out the way I want.

In hope, there is a recognition of an absence of power, or a relinquishing of it.

I cannot affect the outcome, I cannot directly cause it, but as a last resort, I can hope.

If I am hoping to get back together with someone, this implies the decision — the power — is in his court.

All I am doing is waiting for him to impact what happens next.

If what I want is to stop hoping, what I need to do is reclaim that power.

I can do that by making myself the person who decides.

I can decide getting back together is not the right thing to do.

Or I can call him and tell him I would like to, for him to accept or decline.

And then I would know.

I'm Done With Love

After every break up I tell myself I'm through with love.

Then I remember that things don't have to be black and white, in or out, forever or never. There can be a middle ground.

I give myself what I am asking for: a love moratorium. What I need right now is time. Time away from the ridiculous nuisance that is love.

I explore my own interests, learn something new, spend time with friends. I make sure I spend a lot of time alone too. The joy. The freedom.

After some time — a few months, a year, love begins to seem less like a ridiculous nuisance and more like something rather appealing. Radiant, actually. And there is this guy who just told me he wanted to get to know me, and I want to get to know him too.

I give myself what I am asking for: what I need right now is another go at this glorious exuberance that is love.

After Divorce

I really, really like my significant other's involvement.

I like it when he says something that alludes to the fact he read what I wrote that morning.

I like it when I come home from work and he says *"how did your presentation go!?"* which suggests he remembered that it was an important day for me.

I like when I say *"I am going to book a trip to go visit my niece and nephew"* and he says *"Would you mind if I come? I want to spend time with them too".*

Tell me. Does this make me needy?

The answer is, it depends. To someone who does not naturally do these things, I am asking for a lot. To someone with a natural tendency towards getting involved, this is "normal".

After a divorce or a break up you don't necessarily identify negative things about yourself. What you learn instead is that relationships are a system, a system you are both an integral part of, and that life is much easier when what you want is what another person wants to give.

The trick lies precisely in *not* interpreting yourself as flawed, but rather in accepting who you are with resolve, determination and compassion.

Do these things I list above sound like too much for you? If that is so, there is nothing wrong with you. There is nothing wrong with me. We're just not right for each other.

Look, I am not perfect. I am full — and I mean full — of flaws. But looking at it this way completely misses the point.

The biggest, most difficult lessons are these: you cannot change another. Love does not conquer all. And, accept. Accept yourself.

If you do not, a lack of alignment will be the common characteristic you bring into all of your relationships.

Friends Forever

It's about 2:30 in the afternoon and I've talked on the phone with three of my exes just in the course of today. This is because they are my friends.

Let's take a look at why.

When I meet someone who ends up being a significant other it's because I like them as people. (I like them for other things too, but this very fundamental thing is always in place.)

When I am in a relationship with them they are extremely important to me, get to know me really well, become friends with my friends and meet my family. Heck, they become family. This is not something that just evaporates.

When we break up it's not because they were horrible or I was horrible but because the romantic part of the relationship ran its course or evolved and became something else or because we have incompatibilities that mean we cannot live together but can be other things (friends, for example. A team. Accomplices. Coworkers.).

It's a tough world out there. It's hard to find people who have truly seen you through thick and thin, who appreciate who you are, who know you and are there for you.

The last thing I would ever do is throw them away.

No One Better

"I will never find someone better than my ex" is not a mindset. It's a belief. It's a thought — and thoughts are just thoughts. They are not fact. They are not truth. They are possible, but the opposite thought is also possible.

It's possible I will never find someone better than my ex.

It's also possible that there are many, many good men out there, different from my ex, and better for me.

It's also possible that if my ex is my ex something went wrong which is an indication he might be great, but not great for me.

Try on a new, positive thought — an equally plausible one — and see which one feels better.

If the positive one feels better, more hopeful, replace the first one with the second one every time the first one comes up.

Sooner or later you will be open to the possibility that your original belief might be a lie. Because, you know. It is.

Go Alone

So you broke up before that trip you were planning and are now wondering if you should go alone.

Yes, yes, yes. Go alone. Take a notebook. Write things down.

How do you feel? How is it different from what you felt yesterday?

What did you do today that you wouldn't have done if he was here?

Can you see how "you" emerges as "we" fades? Can you do more of "you"?

What are you afraid of? Can you, without putting yourself in harm's way, take more risks, face your fears?

What do you do with the time you would have spent with him? Replace that time with long walks. Discover something. Have meals alone. Discover yourself.

Take pictures. Go to all the romantic places rather than avoiding them. You are kicking off the best love affair, the one that will serve you forever. You are falling in love with yourself.

Remember the time you used to spend searching for the perfect gift for him? Do that for you. Get a massage. Pay for dinner at a fancy place at least one time.

I am not suggesting this trip will be pain free. As a matter of fact it's likely to hurt and remind you of the time you planned it together. But, we can't avoid things just because they are difficult. What you are looking for — your recovery, your identity, your self-esteem — are right on the other side of difficult. Right there, so very close.

Go.

Insatiability

The mark of an addiction to another person is insatiability. It's a ravenous feeling, unquenchable, and you'd do anything for a hit. *I'm just going to call him. I just want to see him.*

Everything else becomes secondary.

It's true that if you are addicted to another person your self-respect vanishes. If I were to put a finer point on that, I'd say that you want something so much you forget about yourself.

Life Happens

Let's say I'm in a relationship and the relationship I am in does not make me happy.

I am lonely even in the presence of this person I am in a relationship with. I am lonely and bored and don't know what to do with my life that suddenly has no spark.

I meet someone else. This other person shimmers so much I feel like I shimmer. This is exciting. It breathes new life into me. This person makes me feel complete and entertained and the spark is back. I am back.

So I leave the relationship that is not making me happy and begin a relationship with this new radiant person.

If we decide to end the story here, then yes. You've got your happy ending.

But the story doesn't end here, because life happens. And suddenly my relationship with the once resplendent person is leaving me wanting. I'm lonely and bored and feel I have lost my way.

Remember when we used to be happy?

If the story ends here, then the ending is not so great. Because I have left in my wake a path of lies and cheating and general destruction. But that's not all.

It finally catches up to me that the problem is me. And that I need to fix me or every single relationship I go into will devolve into me being lonely and bored and lost.

Other people don't fix us. We fix us. If we don't, our type of unhappiness replicates in every relationship. Except sometimes, by the time we find out, it's too late and we realize we are old and our life is ending and we have treated like crap everyone who ever had the audacity to love us.

Is Love Futile?

It would be easy for me to argue that everything, everything is futile, trite and easy to break. Nothing truly produces any result. In a way, it's all useless, like those big life lessons you learn only to make the same mistake over and over.

We are born and we die and someday, not too far into the future, you and everything around you — your mother, your brother, your lover, your child, the streets you walk on, the buildings you work in (on very important things), the stars, the swath of the Milky Way, our galaxy and neighboring galaxies, complete with their geology, their events and their storms — will cease to exist.

To me what this means is that what I am given is its own reward. It means I make the bed because of the pleasure it brings me to see it smooth and tidy — not because I will never tousle it again. (Tousling it, in fact, might be the very best part.)

It means I will be generous and a good friend as often as I can because generosity and friendship are to me full of meaning, not because I'm certain we will never be distant, never go our separate ways into different lives, someday soon forget each other's birthdays.

I didn't know. I didn't know you now have a kid.

It means I will love because I can't not, and because love to me is equal to life — its joy and sorrow and pain and confusion and wonder — not because I'm certain this is going somewhere or because I have a master plan or because we will be together forever, in any form. I can in fact guarantee that we won't be. My heart, you see, is both yours and fickle. I already know you will one day be reduced to a photo I will find at the bottom of a shoe box.

Wow, I loved him so. I wonder where he is now.

Experiences do not come bundled with either purpose or futility. Both those things are up to you.

It Was Awful

After a break up it's really easy to spin out. *He was awful. He never loved me. What a waste of time.*

Thinking this way is really painful. It's not that the thoughts are untrue. It's that it's possible the opposite thought is just as real. *He was wonderful. He loved me. We both learned so much.*

It's just that I suffer a lot less when I realize that if someone spent time with me it was because I mattered to him, and because in his own way he tried as hard as I did.

Things did not work out and that is painful enough. I am hurting enough.

Just because this is over does not mean I have to tear down and destroy everything.

Rebound

Imagine that you live in a comfortable, mostly tidy house. One day, your house gets hit by a natural disaster.

This is the real estate equivalent of a breakup.

What you need to do before the house is ready to be lived in again is fix the house. Is the foundation sound? Is the structure solid? Has this house been remodeled to fit the person you have become after surviving this catastrophe?

A rebound relationship is an attempt to inhabit this house before it has been deemed ready to live in.

Supporting Actors

I have been hurt so, so bad.

Every time I am hurt I learn something new.

I learn, for example, that I can get through this. This, as painful as it is, is something I can survive.

I learn that I want to love more rather than less. I learn that I want to love loudly, eagerly and with courage.

I learn that the only thing that matters are the connections that we make and the most important thing I can do is open my heart rather than close it.

I learn how to take a good look at the situation and recognize the times when really I am hurting myself.

The truth is other people are just supporting actors for all the things I do to myself.

Being hurt has taught me invaluable things and this is why I don't want to forget.

I want to remember.

Scarcity/Abundance

The fear of not being good enough forces an assumption of scarcity.

I am not enough. I don't have enough. Other people who are better than me will take him. Anything he gives to others means less for me.

The energy is grasping, tightening, clenching. It's reminiscent of despair.

Feeling like you are enough assumes abundance. I am enough. I have enough. Other people better than me will enrich him. Anything he gives to others means more for me.

The energy is open, trusting, generous, loving.

How Do You Recover From an Addiction to a Person?

I am not a doctor or a therapist but can instead tell you what works for me.

I ask myself why I am feeling this way and disrelate it from the person.

For example: you are a stand-in for my tendency to want what I can't have. While this feels this is all about you, this has nothing to do with you. This is all me.

To put it in other words, what I am feeling are not feelings for you but my own craving for something that I can only find within me.

I separate feeling something from acting on that feeling. *"I can't help myself"* is a lie. *"I have no control"* is a lie. While it is very, very difficult, I can say *"I want to call you a thousand times just to hear your voice but just because I want to call you a thousand times doesn't mean I am going to call you at all".*

In my experience, this desperate feeling of wanting more of this person has to play itself out, during which time I have to work on myself and uncover why this is happening.

The time that I usually put into a relationship I put into myself instead.

In the meantime, I acknowledge that I do not have to act on what I feel (so I don't feed it) and repeat to myself all the ways this hurts me. At first, telling myself how this hurts me doesn't help at all, but as I repeat it, it begins to sink in.

For example:

It feels like the fix is him but getting a fix (after the initial rush) makes me feel worse, not better. He does not want me. He does not want what I want. He takes all my power and energy away. The sensation that I need him is an illusion and proof of this is that he can't even give me what I'm convinced I need.

I lose my boundaries. I forget about myself.

I need to get myself back, and that is the priority.

I need to learn from this so that it doesn't keep happening, which means I need to focus on understanding why. Where does this come from?

I try not to judge myself for feeling the way I do. Instead I regard what I am going through with compassion.

Finally, if I ever felt like getting myself back felt unreachable, I would consider therapy, or a 12 step program.

Faulty Radar

Let's say, hypothetically, that my father was a womanizer.

That his tendency to systematically cheat had an impact on my upbringing.

Imagine that I was a witness to a pattern that went like this: the glorious, radiant, passionate beginning of a new relationship, followed by fervent promises, followed by broken promises, betrayal and high voltage drama.

Then, the catastrophic severing of the relationship and the instant sprouting of another that had all along been developing in the background.

Now imagine that nearly two decades after my birth the time comes for me to develop my own relationships.

Without intensity things appear pretty drab. Clearly this stable guy who claims to love me but is not into grand gestures is simply not interested enough.

Within expert seduction, impossible promises, crazy reactions and a tendency to lie my subconscious identifies something deliciously familiar.

My reptilian brain — the part that concerns itself only with making sure I'm not in lethal danger— confuses "familiar" with "safe".

To me love is a roller coaster, insane, unstable and agonizing.

I wonder, utterly mystified, why everyone I date ends up trying to deceive me.

My answer is this: my radar has been set wrong. My compass has been set wrong. I know "familiar" but I don't know "healthy". I have never seen healthy. How on earth would I know how to recognize it?

I need to step back. Way back. I don't "move on" straight into the next relationship. Instead I move away from relationships entirely and look at myself and where I come from and consider how I am interpreting what I perceive.

I discover that whenever my heart says *YEAH THIS GUY OMG HE IS THE MAN OF MY LIFE YAAAS* I need to integrate my heart with the rest of me, so that my brain and my gut and every other bit of me can remind her that she has no clue what she is doing.

No, heart. I know it feels this way, but this is not the man of our life. Let's slam on the brakes. Let's know ourselves first. Let's love ourselves first. Look, it's you and me. Let's save ourselves.

"Not lethal" is too low of a bar.

I love myself. I want someone who is for real. You know how I know when someone is for real?

Because love is not supposed to hurt.

If love hurts I need to go recuse myself until I can get my faulty radar adjusted again.

Can a Soul Give Up on Love?

Most definitely.

Said soul resolves it is done. Done with love, forever.

But then the soul gets some distance. It gets some perspective. It restores itself, rebuilds itself, recovers. It mends. It heals.

Somehow, after feeling dry and cracked and empty, spent, this indestructible, beautiful thing reconstitutes itself.

It unfurls. Green, resplendent, enormous.

This is what hearts and souls have in common.

They come back — rejuvenated, revitalized, ready to take a swing at all of it again.

Fear

You can, driven by fear and by ego, break up with your girlfriend before she breaks up with you.

You can walk away from all your relationships, move away from your family, leave all your friends.

You can quit your job before you get fired, and never attempt any creative endeavor. How can something you do be judged or rejected if you never produce it?

Then, you can sit on a raft in the middle of a grey ocean, safe, shielded, isolated from every wonderful thing that could have ever happened for you, aching for all the things that could have been.

Aftermath

Questions to ask yourself after a breakup:

Who am I? Who is "me" without "we"?

What do I like? What do I want? What interests me?

What are the things I set aside when I am in a relationship? Things I've wanted to do or people I want to spend more time with or places I want to go?

Do I have a tendency to pay less attention to my friends, to my endeavors, to myself? How can I resist this in the future?

What happened? Do my relationships end for similar reasons? What are the patterns I would rather not repeat?

How was this breakup my fault? What can I take responsibility for?

Am I usually in a relationship? Do I jump from one to another? What would I need in order to be alone for a while? What would I learn?

How do I define love?

How is my relationship like my parent's relationship?

What hurts?

What do I want to change, do differently?

How do I plan to get there?

Inevitable

I make it a point to remain good friends with the people I once had a relationship with.

Watching them fall in love with someone else is an inevitable part of the commitment I make to myself to keep them in my life.

I won't lie to you. Witnessing someone who used to love me love someone else is a mixed bag. It's sad and painful and wonderful.

It's wonderful because what I want for the people I love is for them to be happy.

It's painful because I want them to love me forever.

I contemplate this feeling. Do I really want someone to love me when I don't love them? Is that my wish for the person that I love, emptiness?

It hurts, for them to move on.

But for them not to would be unbearable.

The Lucky Ones

I am sitting at my dining room table holding and setting down my cup of coffee.

My hands are at my command.

I can't do this with my heart. My heart is not governable.

I love people I shouldn't love, and stop loving people I promised I would love forever. I keep loving people after they say they don't love me, keep loving people long past when we agreed our relationship was over.

Most of the things that vex human beings are related to our ungovernable hearts.

I don't know why this is the case. Why were we made like this? Why were our feelings placed inside us if they are not ours to rule over?

The only possible explanation is that this is what we are here to learn.

It's how we learn how love is worthwhile even when it tears us apart. It's how we learn about pain, ours and that of others. It's how we grow: through the breaking and re-breaking of our hearts.

It's how we learn we can't have something just because we want it. And, that just because we feel something doesn't mean our feelings rule our actions.

It's how we learn other people are not ours to keep. It's how we know it's time to go.

I can love you and keep this love contained and go about my life until this damn love dissipates on its own. It's all I can do — I cannot extinguish it at will.

If I could I would have done so long ago.

I am sorry. You can't. You can't stop loving someone. You have to make the best of this love you carry, and walk the world broken hearted until your heart heals itself.

The good news is that your heart is healing itself even as you read this.

I can leave you with one more thing: the greatest tragedy of all is to go through life feeling nothing. So take all your pain — and I know it's a lot — and as ludicrous as it sounds, thank it. Thank it for existing.

It's us, the broken hearted. We are the lucky ones.

Tonic

Once upon a time there was this guy who turned me on.

I don't mean this just sexually (although, yeah): our interactions felt like a douse, a splash, a tonic. I'd feel my brain light up, fire up, made lists of things I wanted to think about, talk about, felt restless, tossed around half the night; would go off and write up a storm.

A relationship was off limits so these bursts were, well. Inconvenient. Uncomfortable. Distressing. Painful. Tragic.

I felt happy.

To this day I can't classify that no name thing. It would be reductive to point to a chemical reaction — besides, he had this effect on me even when we talked on the phone.

Can chemistry zip through phone lines?

Our interactions were intermittent. This was on me — I didn't know what to make of us so kept trying to find a way to make things fit.

I was bent on preserving something.

Also, I tried to kill it, tame it, cool it off and deny it, mostly to myself.

Every time I managed to wind it down he would make himself present, I suspect deliberately.

Every time he came back, even in the form of a text or call, this sense of being flipped on, like a light switch, would come roaring back, full force.

It was terrifying.

It was amazing.

Here is what he taught me all those years ago: that despite the terror and emotional disruption, this is how I want to live.

That despite the risk and vulnerability I want more of this "on" sensation, rather than less.

At the risk of every anguish and agony, I want my heart wide open.

I don't want to be prudent or reasonable or safe. I don't want to analyze why I might or might not be afraid.

What I want is to live inspired.

Shooting Star

You are not static.

Regardless of your age everything inside you is roiling. We tend to perceive ourselves as rocks or trees, rooted. We are more like fire, like shooting stars in a wide, sparkling trajectory of light.

Everything around you is changing too.

We are unstable sailors trying to keep our footing as we stand on rocky boats.

This means that to subsist we need to constantly recalibrate.

The next time you declare you are lost, think about this. You are not lost. You are finding yourself.

The next time you feel alone realize that this is just sensation, an irrational impossibility if you have yourself.

The next time you feel inadequate or unlovable consider that instead you are learning. You are a student.

And if you are able to regard yourself and realize it was you, your fault, that you were responsible for what happened, then you are also a teacher.

I guarantee you will love again. You will love better precisely because of what you are now learning.

You will be found again, feel connected again, feel beloved again.

I also absolutely guarantee future disorientation, confusion, isolation and heartbreak.

I guarantee you will again fear you will never be loved. You will wonder why you keep making the same mistakes.

At these times, do not despair. Go to the mirror and remind yourself.

I am not lost. I am finding myself. I am not alone — I have me. I am not unlovable or inadequate.

I am already perfect, in a state of necessary, natural recalibration.

Perfect, and forever a work in progress.

I am a shooting star.

About the Author

Dushka Zapata has worked in communications for over twenty years, running agencies (such as Edelman and Ogilvy) and working with companies to develop their corporate strategy.

During this time she specialized in executive equity and media and presentation training. She helped people communicate better through key message refinement and consistency and coached them to smoothly manage difficult interviews with press during times of crisis.

Dushka is an executive coach and public speaker who imparts workshops about personal brand development. She has been hired for strategic alignment hiring, to coach and mentor high potential individuals, improve upon new business pitches, refine existing processes and galvanize a company's communication efforts.

She currently works in executive communications at Zendesk.

Dushka is the author of seven books: "How to be Ferociously Happy", "Amateur: an inexpert, inexperienced, unauthoritative, enamored view of life", "A Spectacular Catastrophe and other things I recommend", "Your Seat Cushion is a Flotation Device", "Someone Destroyed My Rocket Ship and other havoc I have witnessed at the office", "How to Build a Pillow Fort and other Valuable Life Lessons" and "You Belong Everywhere."

The book you are reading, "Love Yourself and Other Insurgent Acts That Will Recast Everything" is her eighth book.

Dushka was recently named one of the top 25 innovators in her industry by The Holmes Report and regularly contributes to Quora, the question and answer site, where she has over 140 million views.

Printed in Great Britain
by Amazon